SIGHT LINES

Page Productions would like to thank British Council and JSW
Foundation for their support.

BRITISH
COUNCIL

Rage Productions would like to thank British Council and JSW
Foundation for their support.

SIGHT LINES
Three Contemporary Indian Plays

First published in 2012 by Hachette India
(Registered name: Hachette Book Publishing India Pvt. Ltd)
An Hachette UK company
www.hachetteindia.com

SRD

ISBN 978-93-5009-441-9

Hachette Book Publishing India Pvt Ltd,
4th/5th Floors, Corporate Centre;
Plot no. 94, Sector 44; Gurgaon 122003, India

Typeset in Adobe Garamond 11/14.5
by RECTO Graphics, Delhi

Printed and bound in India by
Manipal Technologies Limited, Manipal

Contents

Rage & Writers' Bloc

We live in turbulent times. The Indian playwright and Indian playwriting in general is truly in danger of extinction; young writers, tempted by the lucre of television and the lure of cinema, are evading theatre altogether. The few that have stuck to their passion are constantly concerned that their plays will die unperformed on dusty bookshelves. The result – fewer and fewer original scripts. How do young playwrights survive? How do they keep their focus? What impels them to keep honing their drafts, to work on crafting dialogue and characters? How do they keep their dreams alive?

At Rage, we watched the conflict of the young playwright with some interest. And yet, while we were concerned, we were eternally optimistic. The success of Writers' Bloc 1 (2004), Writers' Bloc 2 (2007) and Writers' Bloc 3 (2012) stands testament to our conviction. Writers' Bloc started out as a unique theatre initiative to discover, train and introduce exciting new playwrights to Indian audiences. The sourcing and training of the playwrights and the festival that follows is a collaboration between the British Council, the Royal Court Theatre, UK, Jindal South West Foundation and Rage.

How does the process work? We ask writers to send us their plays – full length, a one act play, even a scene will do. The bottom line – can the writer craft drama?

The result has always been a deluge of scripts from all over India in all languages – English, Hindi, Marathi, etc. – which we, every three years, with the help of our associates, the Royal Court Theatre, London, then sift through to pick about twelve of the most promising writers. Once this is done, the writers are invited to the idyllic Jindal guesthouse in remote Vasind for a series of workshops to interact with some of the finest theatre professionals from Royal Court – April de Angelis, Carl Miller, Elyse Dodgson, Phyllida Lloyd and Ramin Gray. It is here that the participants nurture the germ of their ideas into full length scripts over a span of a year, resulting in a festival where all the plays are performed. Since 2004, 32 original scripts have emerged from the Writers' Bloc stable, including the three that have been chosen for this book. These have been staged to great critical acclaim in India and many countries abroad.

About Rage

The Rage trio – Shernaz Patel, Rahul da Cunha and Rajit Kapur – joined forces in 1993. Our vision statement was simple – '*Do plays without an eye to the box office*'. We opened curtains with an AIDS based double header called *Are There Tigers in the Congo?* The play's fate at the box office was critical acclaim combined with commercial disaster.

In 1996, came a turning point in our journey when we adapted Herb Gardner's comedy *I'm Not Rappaport* for the Indian stage. Re-titling it *I'm Not Bajirao*, this play about two octogenarians fighting to stay afloat in a ruthless urban world caught the fancy of Indian audiences of every age. The result was ten years of performance, 200-odd shows and the birth of a new Indian English dialect in the theatre.

In 2000, we went 'musical'. We staged an ambitious production of Andrew Lloyd Webber's *Jesus Christ Superstar* starring forty actors, dancers and performers.

By 2002, we committed ourselves totally to indigenous theatre with plays like *Class of 84,* a play about seven ex-Xavierites re-uniting, followed by *Pune Highway*, a thriller about testing friendship in extreme circumstances and *Me, Kash and Cruise*, a tale about the changing face of Bombay, over 22 tumultuous years.

Other memorable productions include Girish Karnad's *Flowers,* Anuvab Pal's *Chaos Theory*, and *One on One*, an evening of contemporary Indian monologues.

Our focus over the last ten years has been on modern Indian writing and we have built up a formidable audience following, with many of our plays crossing the 100 and 200 show marks. Rage has not only regaled audiences in India, but also in Amsterdam, Antwerp, Dubai, Germany, London, Malaysia, Seoul, Singapore, Sri Lanka and the United States.

International Playwrights at the Royal Court Theatre

The Royal Court Theatre is Britain's leading national company dedicated to new work by innovative writers from the UK and around the world. The theatre's pivotal role in promoting new voices is undisputed – the *New York Times* described it as 'the most important theatre in Europe'. The Royal Court receives and considers an extraordinary quantity of new work and, each year, presents an ambitious programme in its two venues at Sloane Square in London. In recent years, the Royal Court has also staged productions in New York, Vienna, Sydney, Brussels, Toronto and Dublin. In addition to its high profile productions, the Royal Court facilitates international work at a grass roots level, developing exchanges which bring young writers to Britain and sending British writers and directors to work with artists around the world. The Royal Court Young Writers' Programme also works to develop new voices with a biennial Festival and year-round development work for writers under 26. The Royal Court's success has inspired confidence in theatres across the world and, whereas new plays were once viewed as a risk, they are now at the heart of a revival of interest among artists and audiences alike.

George Devine's 1956 vision of the Royal Court was of a 'truly international theatre' and in the early years of the English Stage Company the repertoire included new plays by writers such as Samuel Beckett, Bertolt Brecht, Max Frisch, Jean Genet, Eugène Ionesco, Arthur Miller and Wole Soyinka. Over the last decade the Royal Court has placed a renewed emphasis on the development and production of international work. By 1993, the British Council had begun its support of the International Residency programme (which started in 1989 as the Royal Court International Summer School) and by early 1996, a department solely dedicated to international work had been created. A creative dialogue now exists with theatre practitioners all over the world including Brazil, Cuba, France, Georgia, Germany, India, Mexico, Nigeria, Palestine, Russia, Spain and Ukraine, and with writers from seven countries from the Near East and North Africa region. All of these development projects are supported by the Genesis Foundation and the British Council.

The Royal Court in India

Since 1996, eight emerging playwrights from India have been participants in the Royal Court International Residency which takes place for one month in London every summer, including Anupama Chandrasekhar who took part in this programme in 2000 and Abhishek Majumdar who came in 2011. This participation has been made possible with the support of the Charles Wallace India Trust.

In January 2001, the Royal Court ran a two week residency workshop for writers from all parts of India organized in collaboration with the British Council and the Artistes Repertory Theatre in Bangalore. The Royal Court team (Elyse Dodgson, Dominic Cooke and April de Angelis) also travelled to Mumbai, Pune and Delhi to investigate expanding the work. Following this, in November 2001, nine of the original playwrights worked with a group of directors on developing their plays with Ramin Gray and Hettie Macdonald. Seven of these plays were shown as part of a festival of new writing in Bangalore in October 2002.

Following the success of this project, Phyllida Lloyd and Carl Miller ran a second residency in Mumbai in September / October 2002, this time in collaboration with Rage Productions. The follow-up of this work was led by the same team in September 2003. In April 2004, nine plays were fully produced as part of the first Writers' Bloc Festival in Mumbai. In June 2005, the Royal Court invited four of the nine writers to work on new plays with us in London. In March 2006, Phyllida Lloyd and Carl Miller returned to Mumbai to work with a new group of writers from all parts of India in collaboration with Rage. Eleven of these plays were produced as part of the second Writers' Bloc Festival in Mumbai during January 2007.

In Spring 2010, the Royal Court returned to India to start a new project with emerging playwrights from all over India, again in partnership with Rage. This work was led by April de Angelis, Elyse Dodgson and Carl Miller. The team returned to India to continue this work in April 2011 and much of this work will be presented in the 2012 Writers' Bloc Festival.

Elyse Dodgson

Elyse Dodgson has been a member of the Royal Court artistic team since 1985 – first, as Director of the Young People's Theatre and, since 1995, as an Associate Director and Head of the International Department. She was the first director of the International Summer School (now the Royal Court International Residency) which she started in 1989, and has produced the Royal Court Young Writers' Festival (1986-91) and the International Season ince 1997. Elyse has co-ordinated play development in many parts of the world including Cuba, Nigeria, Uganda, Mexico, Palestine, Russia, Syria, India and Brazil. She has also edited five anthologies of international plays, all published by Nick Hern Books, from Germany, Spain, Mexico and the Arab World. She was the recipient of the 2004 Young Vic Award and, in 2010, received an MBE for her contribution to 'international theatre and young writers overseas'.

Foreword
Carl Miller

Why on earth write a play in the twenty-first century? Why spend all that time (and it often does take longer than you expect) alone with nothing but your writing materials, piling up sheets of paper that are simply a blueprint for something a bunch of other people might bring to life, converting them to speech, action, movement, light and sound? It's an odd thing to do, yet people have been doing it for centuries in England, where I live, and for even longer in India, where I arrived a decade ago and began to meet the writers in this collection.

I came to India thanks to a remarkable woman called Elyse Dodgson. There is a stereotype of England and its theatre: emotionally repressed, parochial and unable to communicate except through the buried language of subtext. Although Dodgson is one of English theatre's treasures, none of that applies to her. She is passionate, vividly expressive and a visionary advocate of playwriting throughout the world. Maybe that's partly a result of her global roots – as the daughter of Eastern European Jewish immigrants to the United States who made her home in London. But it's even more to do with a personal vision that has transformed the landscape of new theatre writing in England during my lifetime. During the 1990s, Dodgson had introduced a series of extraordinary plays from continental Europe to London audiences through her advocacy at the Royal Court Theatre. As that work became an established part of the repertoire, her quest went ever wider. She was, for example, convinced that there were playwrights in India whose voices audiences in England could be hearing. So she went to India, and persuaded others to come with her. I was one of the people she persuaded and I will always be grateful, although ten years ago I had no idea what I was getting into...

What you can read here gives you an idea of where Elyse Dodgson's idea took us. It has been an inspired adventure rather than a pre-meditated process. There is process, often rigorous process. Among the other theatre artists Dodgson has brought to India are the playwright April de Angelis and the directors Dominic Cooke, Phyllida Lloyd and Ramin Gray. Each of them has shared their way of working with writers formally and informally over the ten years since the work began. It would have been unwise, however, to have started with too rigid a notion of what success would look like for this venture. Would it be for writers who have been part of Writers' Bloc (as the festival of work emerging from these encounters came to be called) to visit the Royal Court Theatre in London; to work on their plays with actors and directors there; to have their plays produced there? Or would success really be for that work to be produced in India? Or for it to go further than one play for Writers' Bloc and be part of a playwright's journey to a body of work? Or for it to be more than a collection of individual successes, but a group of writers, actors, directors all wanting to create thrilling contemporary theatre? Would success be a book like this? It is, and so are all the other examples I've mentioned.

I shouldn't give the impression that these ten years have been a constant stream of sweetness, harmony and international understanding. Some of the most striking breakthroughs have come because of clashes of aesthetics and beliefs. I've returned from each of my encounters with Writers' Bloc writers with my ideas about theatre profoundly challenged and in some way shifted. Those discussions have involved huge, fascinating questions. For those of us working within or against a tradition derived from Aristotelian dramaturgy, the possibility of a conflict-less (or maybe more appropriately harmony-seeking) drama is a challenging proposition. Much mainstream story theory derived from Hollywood relies on the idea of a protagonist pursuing her or his goal in a context that presupposes certain assumptions about the individual and the wider world. What are the incompatibilities (and the possibilities) of work derived from secular theatre practice and religious drama?

There are also continuities, however. I have met playwrights passionate to engage with big questions about the world in which we live, how we live in it, and how to explore those dilemmas truthfully in drama. Playwrights like the trio in this volume, each of whom explores in her or his own way how human beings behave with each other under pressure. All of them pulse with a verve for language, but also an awareness of how slippery it can be. Rather than looking (absurdly, impossibly) for a 'definitive' Indian play, the joy of Writers' Bloc has always been its multiple voices, often contradictory and always contrasting. Each playwright in this book asks different questions in different ways, each with a distinctive set of aesthetic choices.

One of the mind-expanding aspects of working with playwrights away from home is exposure to different languages. Sometimes, completely different – there have been plays in each

Writers' Bloc festival in languages other than English, which have worked brilliantly. But even where English is used, it is an English rooted in India. Commentator Yasmin Alibhai-Brown, talking about Rahul da Cunha's *Pune Highway* describes his characters' use of English in the play as the language 'breaking out and starting out a new trajectory in its unending history'. Da Cunha's writing reflects the magpie vocabularies of characters able to reach for the *mot juste* in a variety of languages and registers. In *Crab*, Ram Ganesh Kamatham hews rhythm and intensity out of contemporary speech, with diction and syntax as tough and sinewy as the physical and mental challenges the characters set themselves, and the world sets them. Farhad Sorabjee's ambitious *Hard Places* reflects a confidence that playwrights based in India (or any country) need not stick only to 'local' or even national questions. This is a play which takes on the world, packed with the rhetorical energy such big questions can demand: a language of philosophy and debate, interwoven with the tense plotting that could power a thriller.

This work has been possible thanks to the generous support of the British Council. There can be no innocent relationship between British institutions and India, given the history of our two countries, and the legacy of the colonial period. It may, however, now be more appropriate to look at those relationships in the context of a new world order which continues to shift the place of both nations in the world. One irony is that the English Stage Company at the Royal Court Theatre is itself a product of changes after the Second World War which profoundly altered Britain's internal and external identity. As Empire disappeared, Britain reconstructed itself with a raft of internal changes. One of these was the development of a system of artistic subsidy through taxation, aiming to make culture not just a luxury but available to all. That made possible the establishment of non-commercial theatres like the Royal Court. It set itself up (sometimes a little self-righteously, maybe) in reaction to a commercial theatre which it regarded as more often than not trivial and parochial. The early years of the Royal Court are rightly famous for their commitment to new British writers, but the theatre also staged plays by Samuel Beckett, Bertolt Brecht, Max Frisch, Jean Genet, Eugène Ionesco, Arthur Miller and Wole Soyinka. Since the work in India began, I have been delighted to see *Free Outgoing* and *Disconnect*, two plays by Chennai playwright Anupama Chandrasekhar, premiered by the Royal Court adding to that International strand in the theatre's repertoire. I met Chandrasekhar on that first visit, and together with the writers represented in this book and at the Writers' Bloc festivals, have learned a huge amount from her about playwriting.

I began this foreword with a tribute to Elyse Dodgson, without whom I would never have met these writers and been lucky enough to witness their unfolding inspiration. I end it with another vote of thanks, to three Indian theatre artists who have taught me so much in the ten years it has been my privilege to know them. Rahul da Cunha is represented in this book by one of his plays, but he is also an impresario and seeker after truth of a kind I feel the early Royal Court would have recognized. Rajit Kapur is a very fine actor, and through his involvement from the very first days of this work has been part of the first readings of extracts from these and many other plays – often called upon to demonstrate a remarkable versatility, from the most poignant scenes of love and loss, to uproarious comedy. Shernaz Patel is no less remarkable a performer – her and Rajit's acting can be dangerously good in a workshop – she acts a scene so well that any writers can believe something she performs by them is a masterpiece. More than that, however, she is a passionate and endlessly committed advocate for the work of these new writers, and an inspiration to me. As Rage, da Cunha, Kapur and Patel have been driving this work with dedication and panache – without them none of this would have happened.

I arrived in India ten years ago from the UK knowing nothing. My horizons are broader thanks to the writers to whom Rage and the Royal Court have introduced me. I hope that you also find something to expand your mind, your heart and your imagination in these three wonderful plays. With their publication I hope there will be productions of these plays all over the world. I also hope it will inspire people to find out more about the work of these three theatrical talents, and that of the other wonderful playwrights creating contemporary drama in India. I also hope that they will inspire other writers, wherever they are, to pursue the strange but vital craft of playwriting.

Carl Miller
October 2011

Introduction
Pragya Tiwari

I almost never know how to begin even the most perfectly thought-out piece. But I persevere and overcome. And when I am done there is still the whole body of it to write. It is hard to say what keeps writers going at their task. They must find the news of the inner world and translate it into words without colleagues or collaborators. They must fashion an immaculate lie to come upon the truth. And the playwright must rely solely on his characters to deliver this truth – create them out of nothing and then 'penetrate the last wrinkle of their souls'.

The task of the playwright is complicated by other reasons as well. Especially, the Indian English playwright. Theatre in India is a marginalized art form that has only barely and feebly outlived its several and enthusiastic obituaries. There is little money and fame to be gotten out of the enterprise. This greatly hinders growth of the art and the artist. State support – monetary and logistical – is all but non-existent and the little that exists is rendered meaningless by bureaucratic red-tape and the lack of well-thought-out policy. Add to this, there are no institutions that offer courses to train potential playwrights in the craft. But the bigger challenge comes from critics who question the very reasons for the existence of Indian English theatre. Can Indian social and emotional realities ever be truthfully depicted in a language that is not inherently Indian? English does not afford the playwright a range of registers for voices across classes and sub-cultures, but for a lot of urban Indians it is not only the language of their intellectual makeup, it is also their first language – the language that they think and dream in. And while their numbers might be comparatively smaller, they constitute a significant segment of people who drive our polity, policies, economics and arts. English brings together Indians divided by hundreds of native languages and dialects and enhances its idea as a cohesive whole. The endeavors of playwrights attempting to document the human history of the nation as it takes place should so be encouraged wholeheartedly.

Plays transform poetry and prose into the spoken word and resound with its energy. They have the power to engage with their audience with immediacy that can grip them, cajole them and move them. They can bring literature down from its pedestal to the common citizen without robbing it of its integral sheen. But the balancing exercises involved in the process are tricky and there is many a slip between the proverbial cup and the lip.

The search for our own idiom has been a long and arduous journey. In fitting irony, the first known Indian English play *The Persecuted*, written a long way before independence by Krishna Mohan Banarjea, was a dramatized debate between orthodox Hindu customs and new western ideas. It took the Indian English playwright a number of decades to break the shackles of imitative colonial English and its later avatar – the Babu English. The early attempts to introduce our own slang on stage, which is admittedly neither as rich nor expansive as its British or American equivalents, were rather awkward. Despite the occasional 'Salaam Sahib' thrown in, the effort remained largely self-conscious and fruitless. Speaking on stage as we do off it, free from the burdens of iconoclasm, is a fairly recent phenomenon. And like the first sentence of a piece, it is but a small step towards a robust Indian idiom that can yield plays that will survive the test of time.

But the search for truth cannot be adjourned for the want of perfection. As Harold Pinter put it in his Nobel Lecture, 'The real truth is that there never is any such thing as one truth to be found in dramatic art. There are many. These truths challenge each other, recoil from each other, reflect each other, ignore each other, tease each other, are blind to each other. Language in art remains a highly ambiguous transaction, a quicksand, a trampoline, a frozen pool which might give way under you, the author, at any time. But the search for the truth can never stop. It cannot be adjourned, it cannot be postponed. It has to be faced, right there, on the spot.'

Indian English playwriting is looking for its own truths and ours, but without colleagues or collaborators. The only concerted effort in this direction in recent times has been the Writers' Bloc workshop organized by Mumbai based theatre group, Rage in collaboration with the Royal Court Theatre, London. Initiated in 2003, this year the workshop ran its third lap. Every three years it invites aspiring and professional playwrights to submit a play and selects a small group from among the entrants to attend a two-week residency at a farmhouse near Mumbai. The majority of these plays are in English but a number of entries in Marathi and Hindi have also become a part of the workshop. During the course of the residency, writers participate in writing exercises, group discussions and avail of individual mentorships to start work on a new idea. In the following months they develop the idea and come back for a second residency to take it closer to completion.

A secluded space cut off from the concerns of everyday life, where you can devote yourself solely to writing, is every writer's ideal. Adding to the charms of this luxury is the presence of a community. Informal after-hours discussions – sharing mutual anxieties and ideas in a virtual haven of inspiration – enhances the writing experience. But for writers used to their alone-ness this can also be a daunting exercise. To be able to defend your work in the face of peer and expert scrutiny and process feedback from diverse perspectives is no short of an act of courage. In that much, the workshop prepares the playwrights for the challenges of the real world while providing them an idyllic head start to their careers. Molds are broken, certainties are questioned and bonds are forged – all of which outlast the time spent at the workshop and the scripts that come out of it. But the most significant role of Writers' Bloc, perhaps, is in providing playwrights access to the final pilgrimage of any script – the stage.

Playwrights, unlike other writers cannot simply appraise their work by revising drafts. To know the worth of what they have created, to be satisfied with it and know it finished, they must know not only how it reads but also how it will look and sound on stage. Aspiring playwrights struggle to find directors or producers to take on their work, let alone a channel to receive feedback for a work-in-progress from within the industry. The Writers' Bloc workshop invites actors to perform bits of the plays being written as part of the review process. The scripts in their final form are taken to some of the best directors and produced for a monthlong festival that runs to packed houses in two of Mumbai's biggest experimental theatres.

Mumbai, the unofficial theatre capital of India, has kept the latter's flag aloft. The city can easily boast of numbers of shows that no other place in India – not even Delhi – can match up to.

But bearing this mast has been no less than bearing a cross. It is so that the city truly deserves an effort like Writers' Bloc. It provides a periodic burst of new talent that has had a desired ripple effect. It has created an ambiance that has been encouraging more and more young people to be a part of the theatre. This is a morale booster for directors who have been struggling to hold on to actors lured away by Bollywood's promise of glamour and money. The domino affect of this change is manifested in other ways as well. Theatre in Mumbai is no longer the bastion of the old guard with unquestionable rules of hierarchy and hand-me-down ideas from the post-independence generation. Its freshly minted democracy and accessibility has the kind of glow that can attract audiences anew. And while it might be too early to announce a renaissance, the excitement is real and palpable and it is dispelling the age-old gloom woven by the unrelenting lack of state support, sponsors, rehearsal and performance spaces.

At the heart of this change are the stories and the reasons why they must be told. Stories that have been bubbling under, distilling meaning from the events of the external world, growing more potent in their confinement. Stories that need to be injected into the chaos of our times lest it overpowers the eternal human spirit.

This selection offers three such stories. Stories that bridge the gap between the personal and the political to take us across the river of reality. History is driven by politics and politics is driven by psychology. The seeds of war are of the same species as duplicity between friends. The tragedy of miscommunication and prejudice; the weakness of the human being and his inherent violence have as much bearing on ordinary lives as they do on the fate of the world. It is in this place, on the aforementioned bridge that the stories here find the bedrock of modern civilization. But their manner has none of the weight of this discovery – it is self-effacing and casual like the veneer of even the most extraordinary days.

Rahul da Cunha's *Pune Highway* takes us into a seedy hotel room where three friends, having just witnessed the gruesome murder of the fourth, are holing up, desperate to escape its consequences. This sudden, inexplicable dramatic tragedy exposes the fears and failures beneath the rehearsed ease of middle-class urban living. The noble dream of friendship, of love nurtured over years is ravaged by a morally ambivalent betrayal – subtle, small and damning. The worst aches are those that stain the air you breathe while evading definition. *Pune Highway* holds a mirror to the fragility of human relationships that conspires with death to render us mortal. Its cloak of humor is a reminder of our cheap rose-tinted glasses that mistake denial for optimism and disregard what is visible but unseen.

Ram Ganesh Kamatham's *Crab* hosts four friends in the process of conversations that elude true communication. His protagonists are younger and their youth tells the tone of *Crab* apart from *Pune Highway*. In the friction between those who fit and those who don't; between those who will be philosophers and those who will be kings lies the existential angst of a new generation; looking for purpose and a safe place for the delicate filigree of emotions threatened by the sharp edges of an increasingly concrete world.

Farhad Sorabjee's *Hard Places* takes the lines we draw between ourselves, the borders we keep with our loved ones to the physically dangerous borders between countries. A family seeks to escape political history but can it escape personal history? The quest to break barriers, to connect, to make a journey and to rise above all that confines us struggles against the limitations of language and the darkness within, diminishing the lines between the macro and the micro.

All three plays are excellent representatives of a new generation of writing in the theatre. Their characters speak, unaffected, in home-grown, lyrical English. Unlike their ancestors they are not mere manifestations of a social or moral message. Instead they look within, taking on the allegations of individualism. Through the prism of the inward eye, these plays reflect on the political, social and philosophical condition of the world we inhabit. They are proud but compassionate; flawed but unafraid, and they will speak to you in many tongues if you let them. I hope you do.

PUNE HIGHWAY

Rahul da Cunha

About the Playwright

Rahul da Cunha started writing plays in 2002. *Class of 84* (2003) traces his years at St. Xaviers College. *Pune Highway* (2004) challenges the bonds of friendship in a severe crisis. Yasmin Alibhai-Brown writing in *The Independent*, London, called the play, 'as powerful and challenging as *Look Back in Anger* must have been in 1956, or Pinter's early work'. *Me, Kash & Cruise* (2008) reflects on 22 years of a changing Bombay. Rahul is writing his first stage musical titled *SING INDIA SING*. His plays have travelled to England, Washington DC, South Korea, Malaysia, Singapore, Amsterdam, Antwerp and Bonn.

Pune Highway

Pune Highway was first presented at the Prithvi Theatre, Mumbai on April 16ᵗʰ 2004, produced by Rage Productions. The cast was as follows:

Nicholas	Bugs Bhargava Krishna
Vishnu	Rehaan Engineer
Pramod	Rajit Kapur
Mona	Yamini Namjoshi
Sakharam	Shankar Sachdev

Director	Rahul da Cunha
Set Designers	Vinesh Iyer & Nikhil Khadilkar
Lighting Designer	Arghya Lahiri & Pushan Kripalani
Sound Designer	Mahesh Tinaikar
Costume Designer	Yamini Namjoshi
Production Controller	Niloufer Sagar

Acknowledgements

I'd like to thank my teacher and mentor, Carl Miller for his guidance through the writing process; my friends and partners, Shernaz Patel and Rajit Kapur, for being great friends and fab partners and my stellar cast – Bugsy, Reh, Rajoo, Yams, Shanks and Ash (Ashwin Mushran) – for making my words truly their own and bringing the play to life.

Playwright's Note

Pune Highway was conceived one morning in September 2003. My mentor Carl Miller's invaluable insight had been resonating in my head – '*Read the daily newspapers, hundreds of story ideas will spring out at you.*'

The *Times of India* reported a brutal stabbing on the Mumbai–Pune Expressway. Four young bankers, faced with the terrible dilemma of saving either a friend or themselves, from a gang of highway robbers, chose the latter. It seemed like a perfect set-up for a play – an emotional roller-coaster ride of guilt, fear and terror, over a 90 minute time line.

I looked at the play at two levels. First, as a pure psychological thriller – how do childhood friends react especially when confronted with a serious crisis? But I thought of layering it with a couple of larger sociological issues – how far can a crisis bring up the worst instincts of greed, disloyalty and betrayal in a consumptive society? Have we become more ruthless as human beings, forced to think only about our own survival?

In the course of writing, I explored a new kind of language – a much coarser, modern dialect. My characters swore at one another, conversed in crass Hindi and Indianized English, talked of extramarital affairs, all the while attacking each other's shortcomings while hiding their real selves from each other. Audiences in India were quite shocked at a play that was so colourful in language and so coarse in characterization and subject. The play travelled subsequently to London, where Yasmin Alibhai-Brown writing in *The Independent*, London, had this to say – '*Playwright Rahul da Cunha exposes the degeneracy of contemporary, moneyed Indian society. The crude, pared down English lacks compassion or grace and becomes a metaphor for India's fast, thoughtless and furious globalization. It is as powerful and challenging as John Osborne's* Look Back in Anger *must have been in 1956, or Pinter's early work. It is English again, breaking out and starting out a new trajectory in its unending history.*'

I'd like to think I've created a few interesting, but ordinary people, faced with an extraordinary situation.

Cast

Nicholas Thomas	A stammering Salsa teacher
Vishnu Mathur	An ex-coke addict; Merger & Acquisition specialist
Pramod Khandelwal	A wheeler dealer
Mona	Pramod's girlfriend
Sakharam	A waiter

(5 a.m. A seedy hotel room on the Bombay-Pune Highway. In the darkness we hear this conversation. It's in a car. The sounds of rain and swishing of car wipers. Music blaring from the car stereo.)

Babu   Oh God! Switch the bloody station…

Vishnu   Yes dude… bloody Hindi music…

Pramod   You guys are bloody total *firangis*. This is our bloody culture…

Vishnu   Culture my ass, Khandu. You call remixes culture?

Babu   Total rip-off. These fucking filmy companies keep stealing English songs…

Pramod   I don't want to argue with you guys…

Vishnu   You have better things to do, *huh*?

(Vishnu and Babu start laughing. Then suddenly they see something and shout)

Vishnu   What's that?

Babu   Watch it, Nicky!!

Pramod   Hey Nicky, stop the car!

(The car screeches. The sound of thunder. And then silence. A large neon misspelt HOTEL MOONLIGT can be seen from outside the window. Green walls, the whoosh of large trucks passing on the highway, the headlights keep flashing through the windows. Four tube lights illuminate the room. The song 'Baath Ban Jaye' from QURBANI, plays from a distant radio. Two men are in this room. Nicholas Thomas, 40, sloppily dressed, lying on the bed. Vishnu Mathur, 35, dressed in suit and tie, with his back to the audience keeps opening and closing a silver Zippo lighter with maddening regularity)

Nick   Vishnu man, stop that, you're d-d-driving me mad,
            man!! I can't think!! This is crazy! I've got pins and
            needles in my ass, man. Where the f-f-fuck is Pramod?
            What's taking him so long? The bugger just takes
            off... doesn't tell us where he's going. Did he tell
            you anything, Vish... Vish... *Vishnu*, man... b-b...
            bloody open your mouth... and say something, man!!!
            (No answer, beat) Where the f-f-f... fuck are we...
            HOTEL MOONLIGT... What the hell is *MOON*...
            Oh man, they mean Moonlight... light is spelt *l, i, g,
            t!* (Hears two people in the next room having sex)

Man   *Hey rani... abhi kya soneka hai... ek hi ghaanta bacha
            hai..*

Woman   *Toh?*

Man   *Eh idhar aa na... rani.*

Woman   *Nahi abhi nahin...*

Man   *Aaja rani... ab* mood *ban raha hai...*

Woman   *Nahi nahi... abhi to kiya na, teen baar...*

Nick   *(shouts)* Oh, you two stop that in there... we can't
            think in here!!!

*(Sharp knock, Nicky switches on the tube lights, opens door. A third
man, Pramod Khandelwal, aged 45 hurries in)*

            Where were you, man... you said you'd be back
            immediately... We've been sitting here... sweating
            like p-p-pigs... the b-b-bloody power keeps going...
            just look... look at those f-f-frigging bulbs, the hot
            water tap in the bogs gives cold water, the cold water
            tap gives brown water. Man, you should try staring at

a painting of a half naked village chick, with a *matka* on her head for one hour… the carpet smells of rat poison … and you… you just d-d-disappear, like the f-f-friggin Invisible Man… leaving us holding our d-d-d… What's going on, man?

Pramod   So what's your question?

Nick   *Huh*?

Pramod   Nicky, piss off… I need to think.

Nick   He needs to think! Did you hear that, Vish?!! Mr. Rodin needs to think!

Pramod   Yes I do.

Nick   And what are we… just part of the furniture, *huh*? Where were you?

Pramod   Unlike you, I was out trying to fix things…

Nick   F… fix things. What are you… a f-f-fucking carpenter?

Pramod   Yes, I'm a fucking carpenter…

Nick   Did you get the car fixed?

Pramod   Are you nuts?! It's 5 in the morning… this is the highway… there is no garage or mechanic for miles…

Nick   What about getting a cab?

Pramod   This isn't Churchgate Station, where you just call one…

Nick   And the ambulance…?

Pramod   There's a vague cell number. What d'you do with a cell number?

Nick	Did you contact the cops?
Pramod	The cops… ever tried contacting the cops… they never pick up the bloody phone.
Nick	Man, you should keep trying…
Pramod	Look… I will call them, later. They're probably all asleep anyway. Stop asking so many questions…
Nick	I'll stop asking them, when you start answering them. Oh man, Khandu, they're soon going to find Babu's b-b-body, just lying on the highway… blood pouring out… they're going trace it to us…
Pramod	How will they trace it to us?
Nick	I don't know… they have their ways, man, they're cops.
Pramod	Relax… you're just panicking… let the grown ups handle this.
Nick	*I'm panicking*? The longer you take to call anyone, the more you're going to screw us. I'm calling them…
Pramod	I said we will call… not just yet…
Nick	Vishnu, what's with this Charles Sobhraj shit?
Pramod	We will wait till daybreak…
Nick	Wait till *daybreak*…? Who do you think you *are*… *General Patton*?
Vishnu	Pramod, cut this annoying cloak and dagger routine, *okay*?
Nick	F-f-fuck, finally Rip Van Winkle speaks…

Pramod	Look, anyway... what are you going to tell the cops? We don't have a clear, plausible story...
Nick	*(aghast) Plausible story*??? What clear p-p-p-plausible story... we didn't do anything wrong!
Pramod	Cops, man, cops. They terrify the shit out of you. Staring through their one-way mirrors!
Nick	*(small beat)* They don't have one-way mirrors...
Pramod	*What?*
Nick	They don't have one-way mirrors, in a police chowki on the Bombay Pune highway...
Pramod	Don't get technical, Nicky...
Nick	Anyway we d-d-don't need to make anything up... It's quite clear to me what happened. You were sitting in the car... I was there in the centre of the action.
Pramod	You... clear to *you*?
Nick	Yeah, me! To me... got it... *(Pramod laughs)* Why the f-f-fuck you laughing, man, why you laughing?
Pramod	*(imitates him)* '*It's quite clear to me what happened!!!*' Mr. C-C-C-Confident.
Vishnu	Hey, don't make fun of him!
Nick	Yeah... f-f-fuck you.
Pramod	Tell them your version of what happened, they'll fling us in the slammer and throw away the key.
Nick	That's rubbish...

Pramod	Anyway, why are you in such a hurry to go to the cops... Three rich Bombay boys... in a Mitsubishi Lancer; they'll have us for breakfast...
Vishnu	What's biting your ass about the cops, man?
Pramod	Don't forget what they did to all of us last year...
Nick	*Ya*... but we were p-p-parading nude on Marve beach, man, what d'you expect? Here we're innocent!
Pramod	Don't forget the stabbing, Nicholas... you were next to him when they knifed him.
Nick	And where were you during this whole incident... climbing the f-f-fucking Himalayas, I suppose? You were the son of a b-b-bitch issuing instructions!! Why did we stop in the first place...?
Pramod	We didn't know that it was a trap. Any human being would have stopped if they saw a body lying in the middle of the road.
Nick	But it wasn't a body!!
Pramod	But it looked like one at that distance.
Nick	Why didn't we just drive past? There was enough space. You wanted to f-f-fucking stop!!! *You* said stop, not me, not Vishnu, not Babu... *you!*
Pramod	Nicky, it's too late for pointing fingers, we have to be united on this.
Nick	No, Pramod, it's not too late. You never t-t-take responsibility for your actions?! You screw up and when the shit hits the ceiling, you b-b-b-bloody bail

out, man! *(small pause)* We're all responsible for Babu's stabbing...

Pramod   We're not responsible... you're getting emotional... again... Nicky... it was an unexpected accident...

Nick   F-fuck! You justify everything. Empty words... no action. *(To Vishnu)* Vish... he's a chicken shit coward. But you... what happened to you? I was screaming at you... to come and help us. But you just sat there, man... you just s-s-sat there.

Vishnu   Yes... I did.

Nick   Why?

Vishnu   I have no excuses... Nicky. I failed Babu. I failed you. You're just never prepared for such things.

(small beat)

Pramod   Nicky, he was dead...

Nick   How do you know... they attacked both of us... but I'm alive, right?

Pramod   You ran, Nicky. You were lucky to get away. He wasn't.

Nick   We should've gone back for Babu. We could have pulled him into the car.

Pramod   They stabbed him repeatedly.

Nick   Babu was a big guy... tough... he could take solid pain...

Pramod   No one could withstand that level of punishment.

Nick   You wanted to zip off. Thinking only of your bloody self.

Pramod Nick, if we'd gone back to get Babu, they would have nailed us all.

Nick Bollocks!!!

Pramod It was either getting Babu, or saving all our asses.

Nick *Crap*!!

Pramod It was a judgement call, *okay*!

Vishnu *But the wrong one, Pramod... Too busy being blown by your babe in the back seat, you horny fuck!! (Knock on the door. They stop.) Kaun hai?*

VOICE *Chai ka* order...

Pramod *(to them)* Did either of you guys order tea?

Nick N-n-no *(Vishnu shakes his head)*

Pramod *Hamara* order *nahin hai... Doosra* room *ka hoga.*

(Harder knock. Pramod opens door. A dirty, unkempt waiter, with a filthy tray of tea, scratching his ass, yawning.)

Waiter *Aaah ha ha... garma garam chai leke aaya... (puts tray down on the table) Bola... kasa ahes tu... bara?*

Vishnu Hello... and you are?

Waiter *Mee? (a la film actor Rajesh Khanna) Aaya Ram, gaya Ram, pan mee* Sakharam.

Vishnu Oh man, stand up comedy at 5.30 am...

Pramod Hey Boss, *hum bola tumko, yeh hamara* order *nahin hai... kuch* mistake *hoga.*

Waiter *Mistook nahi... room teen shey teen se pone aala. (Waiter picks up bill and reads the contents)*

Vishnu	Maybe he can't understand you, Pramod... maybe you should try sign language?
Waiter	*(reads)* '*Chai tees rupya... doodh daah rupya... aani shakar, paach,* tax extra...'
Nick	They charge for the *s-s-sugar?*
Pramod	*Boss, maine bola ek bar,* please *wapas leke jaana.*
Waiter	*AYGA... kayko tang karta mala... subah paach baje aahe... main akela hai... iss hotal madhi* lift *nahin hai... kisi ne yeh* room *se pone kela...* Manager *bola.*
Pramod	*Nahi,* boss
Waiter	*Nahi?* (wicked smile) *Koi aur aahe* room *madhi? Kuch 'ladis wadis'?*
Nick	*(losing his temper)* Yeah, mother f-f-f... your Mom is bathing in the loo...
Waiter	*Kai...?*
Vishnu	Nicky relax...
Waiter	*(imitates Nick)* 'Mom bathing in loo!!' *Eh... Bhau... Marathi sanga.*
Nick	*(tries Marathi) Tujha* mother... *(to Pramod)* Hey, what's Mom in Marathi...?
Pramod	*Aai...*
Nick	*Tujha Aai... sandaas... snaaning...*
Waiter	*(very amused) Eh, eh Bhau, tumchi Marathi changli aahe... wah wah wah...*

Nick   (*sarcastic*) Okay… *thamba*… let me look. You don't believe me, right?… Let's check the room together. Maybe there are some really small people who never checked out. (*Nicky first looks under the bed*) *Nako… Nako*… no one in here. No one hiding here (*goes up to table, opens tea pot, looks inside*) See no one here either. (*screams at him*) *Abhi niklo,* asshole! No one ordered the tea, got it!

Vishnu   (*giving waiter a tenner*) *Bhai saheb, theek hai. Rehne do.*

Waiter   (*pointing at Nicky*) *Yeh* Sunny Deol *ko bolo… aaram se baat karne ka… garam hone ka phaayda nahin hai.*

Vishnu   *Main boloonga*… thank you… (*opens door*) much obliged, take care… love to the family… (*Waiter exits*)

Pramod   (*grabs Nick*) Nicholas… Nicky look at me… you get your act together okay…? You're going seriously ballistic!

Nick   I hate these guys… their attitude just s-s-sucks.

Vishnu   Put the '*Do Not Disturb*' sign on the door, man…

Nick   What '*Do Not Disturb*' sign? The restaurant in this frigging place is spelt '*DINNING HALL*', and you expect them to have a *DO NOT* b-b-bloody *DISTURB* sign?

Pramod   Vish, what's with this waiter guy, you think?

Vishnu   I don't know… but I didn't much care for his vibe.

Nick   *Vibe*? Who are you, *Buddha*?

Pramod	I don't think he made a mistake with the order.
Vishnu	You need to take a chill pill, my friend…
Nick	Hey guys… no offence… but I am in the room, *ya*? Don't you want my views… my advice?
Vishnu	*(ignoring Nick)* Did you talk to anyone else, Khandu?
Pramod	At five in the morning…??
Nick	Okay, thanks, I'll give you my views anyway. I think it's the fat punk at the reception…! He gave me a look, when we arrived… as if he knew we had done something. He asked me how long we were staying for.
Vishnu	Nick, all hotel receptionists have to ask that question…
Nick	I'm telling you, these guys know something. That hotel guy sent this waiter to check up on us… did you look at his eyes?
Vishnu	No, I never do that with a guy.
Nick	Maybe… they're working with the cops… what are they called… informants?
Pramod	Nicky, don't get all Hindi movie on me! *(a beat)*
Vishnu	*(a thought strikes him)* Khandu…
Pramod	*Ya*…?
Vishnu	Where's the babe…?
Pramod	Which *babe*?

Nick	The babe you were c-c-c... *(looks to Vishnu for help)*
Vishnu	*(helping him)* Cuddling? *(Nick shakes head)*... caressing? *(Nick shakes head, frustrated)* ...coochie cooing?
Nick	*(nods)* Yeah... coochie cooing in the back seat of my car...
Pramod	Who, Mona? I don't know...
Nick	What d'you mean you don't know? We all came here t-t-t... together... you asked us to hang in here... and then you left with her...
Pramod	She got a lift... she's headed to her old man's pad in Lonavala or somewhere.
Nick	How did she get a lift?
Pramod	I flagged down a car... nice old Parsi couple... they were headed in that direction...
Vishnu	Why did you pack her off?
Pramod	I thought that was the best thing to do.
Nick	Best thing to do...?
Pramod	Look, I don't want her to get involved in all this... best to leave chicks out of this.
Vishnu	Pray why?
Pramod	We're in deep shit as it is, Vishnu... a chick in our hair just now will, you know... create unnecessary complications.
Nick	How...?

Pramod	Oh man… women are hysterical… they panic under pressure. Not like us guys. Anyway, why are you asking so many questions about her…?
Vishnu	Largely because she was there when Babu was stabbed. She is strictly speaking a witness. How d'you know she won't open her mouth?
Pramod	To *who*…?
Vishnu	To the cops… to her Pop… to her beautician… I don't know… how well do you know her…?
Pramod	Well enough, trust me…
Nick	Trust you… *Hah,* that's a g-g-good one !!!
Vishnu	Khandu, tell me about the girl…?
Pramod	What do you want to know?
Vishnu	We could start with her birthstone… then move onto other more relevant info… but I don't think we have the time.
Pramod	Look, she's just someone I met at a disco last week… turned out she freaks on horse racing too… so we got talking.
Nick	You've known this c-c-chick only a week… and already you're riding her.

(cracks up at his own joke, they give him a dirty look)

Vishnu	So you're serious about this babe… or what?
Pramod	No man! Why am I being asked all these questions…?
Vishnu	Because I'm not the guy with the James Bond lifestyle.

Nick	Khandu, I've always told you… your weakness for the chicks, man… will one day be your Waterloo. *(Vishnu impressed with Nick's use of language)*
Pramod	Nick… it's too early in the morning for lectures, *okay*? This is just a casual affair… A man must do what he has to do…
Vishnu	'*A man must do what he has to do*'. Dude, you should write the *HALLMARK* greeting cards.
Nick	Anyway, the way you guys were n-n-necking today, didn't seem casual to me… Oh no… ho ho ho. You know what I'm thinking, Vish?
Vishnu	No idea, Santa Claus.
Nick	Maybe Pramod's slut is behind this whole thing…
Pramod	Nicky, stop calling Mona a slut, got it, or I'll *jhaap* you!
Nick	Why… she is a slut… c'mon look at her…
Pramod	Ah, but you would still never get her.
Vishnu	*Just can it, you two*…! Pramod, can we establish a series of events here? You dropped us here, hitched your ladylove with two friendly Zarathustrians… and *then*?
Pramod	I… *uh*… walked some distance looking for help… clear my head.
Vishnu	You were away an hour…
Pramod	Things take time… Vish.
Vishnu	Khandelwal, I might look stupid… but deep down I'm quite bright.

Pramod	Okay, I made some calls…
Vishnu	How, I'm not getting a signal.
Pramod	There's a public phone down the road.
Nick	To *who*?
Pramod	Some people…
Vishnu	Pramod, man!!
Pramod	Okay… okay… I wanted to find out about the cop situation here… I wanted a name… a contact… who's the main cop, that kind of thing.
Nick	This is a real balls up…
Pramod	Oh c'mon Nicky, just shut your dumb Catholic ass…
Nick	(*beat*) *Syrian Christian*, you ignorant toad…
Pramod	What?
Nick	I'm not Catholic… I'm S-S-S-Syrian Christian.
Pramod	What's the *difference*…?
Vishnu	We've known each other twenty years, and you think he's *Catholic*…?
Pramod	*Ya*. He goes every Sunday to Church, *na*?
Nick	You're really a moronic Bania, you know that…
Pramod	(*angry*) *Maadu*… I'm a *Maadu*.
Nick	*Ya*, but you're a Hindu, *na*?
Pramod	I'm from Rajasthan… ever seen a map?

Nick   *Ya ya ya…* but you're a Hindoo, *na…*

(They are interrupted by the couple having sex next door)

Nick   *(shouting at them)* Hey just stop it in there, why don't you find another room or hotel…

(The lady in the next room yells at Nick, cutting him off)

Lady   *(offstage) Abe… tereko bajaneka hai toh idhar aake baja na… darwaze ko kya baja rahe ho (she laughs at him mockingly, Nick at a loss for words, Vishnu laughs and the phone rings)*

Pramod   *(picks up phone)* Hello… *(no one answers)* Hello…

Nick   Who's it?

Pramod   Hello… *hello (to them)* No answer… just some crackling sounds.

Vishnu   How would anyone know we're here…?

Pramod   Probably a wrong number…

(Puts the receiver down, it rings again, this time Vishnu picks it up)

Vishnu   Hello… hello… *(cups phone, to Pramod)* There is definitely someone at the other end. I can feel it… really feel it.

Nick   You're feeling an aura through the phone, *Swamiji*?

Vishnu   Hello… hello!!!

Nick   I'm telling you it's that slime ball waiter… let me give him a piece of my mind. *(Nick grabs phone, entangles around Vishnu, yells into it)* You waiter guy, Sakharam or whatever the shit your name is… I know it's you…

Pramod	He doesn't speak English, *ya*!!
Nick	*Hum t-t-t… tereko… .uhm… box… thappad… jhaapad dega…* (caller hangs up) Hello… hello… hello!!! (to them) He hung up…
Vishnu	(laughing) I don't blame him… Nick, your Hindi is awesomely frightening…
Pramod	They didn't teach you Hindi in school?
Nick	I switched to French.
Vishnu	Man, you know who this reminds me of…?
Pramod	Who?
Vishnu	Mr. Fonseca. From our building.
Pramod	That third floor guy? Vish… you think of the weirdest things… man.
Nick	He was that ugly horny lech, *right*…? Two t-t-tufts of hair sprouting out of either ear…
Pramod	Remember the time we rang his doorbell and Madame Thabela's?
Nick	Who's Madame *Thabela*?
Pramod	You had left the building. She was this fat babe who moved in opposite Fonseca…
Vishnu	She always wore a dress two sizes smaller…
Pramod	Looked like a *pukka* Kamatipura Madam.
Nick	Her name was Madame *Thabela*…?
Pramod	No, man… pet name… for obvious reasons.

Nick	So what did you guys do?
Vishnu	One Sunday morning, Khandu, Babu and I… we rang both their doorbells simultaneously, scooted down the landing and hid.
Pramod	Same time *darwaza khola dono ne.*
Vishnu	Obviously she thought that she's caught our horny dude in the act.
Pramod	And then, magic *se,* his pyjama *naada* comes loose.
Vishnu	*(small pause, suspense)* Down come the pyjamas… and Madame Thabela is exposed to the Leaning Tower of Pisa… in all its morning glory!
Pramod	You could hear her scream all the way in Malad…!
Vishnu	Khandu and I split, assuming Babu was behind us…
Pramod	But he slipped… and fell…
Vishnu	And they were on him. How they *jhaaped* him… Fonseca and Thabela. Hitting and hitting him. And we just watched… helplessly.

(All three pause with this memory, realizing the immediacy of what has just happened. A sharp knock on the door, they don't hear it initially. Knock again)

Pramod	*Kaun hai?*
Waiter	*(singing at the top of his lungs)* 'Andheri raaton mein… Sunsaan raho par'

(Pramod opens door. Waiter enters)

Waiter	*Din mein aapka* waiter *lagthaa hoon… naam hai Dipti* Manager Sakharam…

Nick	What's going on here… if it isn't humping couples, it's asshole waiters.
Pramod	*Kya chahiye?*
Nick	I'm telling you Pramod… Vish… this waiter guy is a mole… they're trying to mess with our brains…
Pramod	Nick… relax… I'll handle this… *Kisne bheja tumko?*
Vishnu	Guys… guys… relax… he's just trying to bait us.
Waiter	*Tum log… khub* tension *main lagta hai, kya baat hai?*
Nick	Take a walk fucker!
Waiter	*Kya?*
Pramod	He doesn't know English, Nicky…
Nick	*Tum yahan se paidal jao!*
Waiter	*Accha… accha… aaram se… gabru nako… (to Pramod) Tera maal aaya re maal.*
Pramod	*Maal? Kya maal?*
Waiter	*Maal… maal… bahut keemti maal… Quality (indicates girl)*

(A young girl, Mona rushes in. Throws arms around Pramod)

Mona	Oh Prameeee!!!
Nick	*(to Pramod)* Rabaart, it's your Mona darling…!!!

(Waiter eyes girl. Mona gives him a withering look. She gives him a Marathi gaali. 'Hadh'. He exits singing)

Mona	Oh Prammy… I'm so scared… just hold me, please…

Pramod	Mona, what are you doing here… the last I saw you, you were in a car…
Mona	I couldn't leave you. I, like, asked those sweet people to drive me back here, Prammy. *(Vishnu and Nick hide a smile)*
Pramod	*(embarrassed)* Mona, please don't call me Prammy?
Mona	Why?
Pramod	Just don't, okay!
Mona	Alright, Prammoo…
Pramod	Why did you come back??
Mona	You don't want me here?
Pramod	I didn't say that. Did you call anyone?
Mona	Why are you asking me all these questions…? You're so nervous, Prammy.
Pramod	…I'm fine
Mona	I don't think so…
Vishnu	Mona, he's cool. He just watched a good friend being repeatedly stabbed. No big deal.
Mona	Prammy, you think I'll blab about what happened… you don't trust me?
Pramod	Of course I trust you. But did you call anyone, tell anyone what happened?
Mona	No… Prammy. My lips are sealed… I don't want you to get into trouble… *na?*

Pramod	What do you mean get into trouble?
Mona	What…?
Pramod	You said you don't want us to get into trouble… what do you mean…?
Mona	I don't know, I just said it… this is a different place… not like Bombay… things work differently.
Pramod	Mona… talk straight *ya*…
Nick	F-f-fuck, man… this woman plays solid games… Vish, you should hire this babe to negotiate your toughest deals.
Mona	*(sidles up to Nick)* Nicky, what's your problem with me… you don't like *women*?
Nick	Oh no… I like women… I just d-d-don't like you…
Mona	He's so cute…
Pramod	Mona, seriously… I told you to go, get the hell out of here.
Mona	*Ya*… Prammy I know… you said I'd be safer… away from you… away from all this tension… but I was spooked… I didn't know where else to go.
Pramod	What happened to your Dad's place in Lonavala…?
Mona	I changed my mind.
Pramod	Why?
Mona	My Dad is there… I forgot he was going there for the weekend.
Pramod	So?

Mona   He goes there quite often… with *uh*…

Pramod   With *who*…

Mona   He has another wife. My Mom knows about this woman. Actually my Dad has three wives. Also he would ask me too many questions. '*Why are you out so early in the morning…, Why are you alone?*' I would have to tell him the full story… and you don't want that, *na*?

Pramod   *Uh*… no not yet. (*Suddenly Mona holds her stomach, retching, she runs to the toilet*) What's wrong with your stomach, Mona?

Vishnu   Pramod… what the sweet Jesus is going on?

Nick   Why is she v-v-v-vomiting, Prammy?

Pramod   I don't have a clue, man…

Nick   You've known this babe a week and she calls you P-P-P-Prammy?

Vishnu   …Khandu tell me something…?

Nick   Is she f-f-f… fucking pregnant?

Vishnu   That was my question… though I would've put it more tastefully.

Pramod   What am I, her bloody gynac?

Vishnu   Pramod… man… now would be an appropriate time to tell us all your sordid secrets (*embarrassed silence by Pramod*) Khandu… you old dipstick… have you really known Mona the Terrible for a week? (*guilty silence*) Okay… your silence is revealing. Is this sleazy affair of yours marginally longer or much longer than a week? Pick one.

Pramod About... *uh*... a month

Nick A month!!

Vishnu I will repeat my question...

Pramod Okay, okay... about two months... maybe more.

Nick (*imitating Pramod*) '*Just someone I met at a disco a few days ago*'. Why the f-f-fuck you lying to us?

Pramod A guy like you would never understand...

Vishnu Pramod... please don't tell me that you have generously deposited some of your unprotected sperm into her?

Pramod Vishnu, talk English... you mean am I the father...? How the hell do I know?

Nick But surely you were the only guy b-b-bonking her? How can a stud like you share your babe with anyone else?

Pramod Look, I don't know anything about her... who she's been with... we've been out a few times... you know how it is?

Vishnu No... not really... (*Mona returns, they go to a corner*)

Pramod (*to Mona*) Are you alright?

Mona I just want some water.

Pramod (*to Vishnu*) Water...

Vishnu (*to Nick*) Water...

Nick *Huh?*

Pramod Water *ya*...

(Pramod pours her some water, they're staring at her while she drinks)

Mona What... what are you looking at... Prammy, why are they all staring at me...?

Pramod *(beat) Uh* Mona... are you...?

Mona What? Am I *what*?

Pramod You know...

Mona A cross dresser... a Cancerian... a fitness instructor?

Vishnu I like her... she's funny.

Pramod *Uhm*... are you...?

Mona Just ask the question, Prammy...?

Vishnu *(getting impatient)* Mona, Marwari boys cannot ask straight questions. He wants to know why you were vomiting... is it something major like some bad food you ate last night... or merely that you are carrying his child... his *bastard* child? *(to Pramod)* That's what you wanted to know, *right*, Prammy?

Pramod *Uh*... thanks Vish... yes... appreciate it... always found your directness very refreshing, man.

Mona *Yes* Prammy... we are... pregnant.

Vishnu Congratulations... Prammoo.

Pramod And who... who is the...?

Mona *Duh*, dude... you of course...

Pramod *Me*...?! How do you know...?

Mona	Prammy, You think I just sleep around? You think I'm that kind of girl?
Vishnu	Nope. Mother Theresa herself.
Mona	I've been faithful to you... for the last few months.
Pramod	But why didn't you tell me...?
Mona	Tell you what??
Pramod	That you weren't... weren't taking any... *uh*...
Mona	You know, all you guys are the same... why didn't you wear a...
Nick	Man, I've had it with this 'fill in the blanks' shit... talk straight *ya*... *'Are you... a... why didn't you wear a...'* we're all adults here.
Mona	I'm sorry, Nicky, but we are all not as forward as you...
Vishnu	You could have fooled me.
Pramod	Thanks Vish. Mona, you know you were taking a real chance?
Mona	And you weren't?
Pramod	Who else knows?
Mona	You're so frightened. Silly, no one except you... and now them of course...
Pramod	This is such a cock up. *(a beat)* Mona... you're going to have to have... a... a...
Nick	Man... here we go again!!

Pramod   Shut up!

Mona   Have *what*? An abortion... no way...

Pramod   Mona... we can't... we can't have this child...

Mona   Why not...

Pramod   We just can't...

Mona   It's not your decision. I'm having it, not you. I want this child.

Pramod   Mona, why do you want to have this child so badly?

Mona   Don't you like kids... *huh*, Prammy? Tell me... don't you want to have kids...?

Pramod   *Uhm*... of course... Mona... I can't *(struggling with words)*... look I can't help... *uh*... support... shit... this is sounding all wrong.

Vishnu   It most certainly is.

Mona   Prammy... how can you not accept your responsibility...? *(points to her stomach)* This is, like, 50 % your creation... what were you thinking?

Pramod   Look, just stop with your games okay...

Mona   This is not a game, Pramod...

Pramod   What d'you expect me to do... you spring this news on me...

Mona   I want you to accept your responsibility

Pramod   What *responsibility...?*!!

Mona	You wanted to have your fun. You did. But when pay up time comes… you want to run away. All you guys are the same…
Pramod	I'm not running away…
Mona	Anyway Pramod, this is entirely my decision… to have the baby… if you don't want to accept this child as yours… what can I say… you will just have to face the consequences.
Pramod	Oh screw you… Mona… *(she glares at him)* Sorry. Look, for God's sakes, don't lay this guilt number on me… this whole thing started off as a casual thing for you too… where are you going with this…?
Vishnu	Straight to the cleaners.
Mona	Pramod, just remember… this scene was never casual for me…
Pramod	So are you going to tell your Dad?
Mona	You're mad? Only after we're married. You don't know my old man. If he finds out about this, he will kill me… and *you*.
Pramod	*Me*…? Why me…?
Mona	I am his only daughter… his angel.
Pramod	But he doesn't have to find out about your pregnancy…
Mona	He doesn't have to… but he will… c'mon Prammy…
Pramod	*How*?

Vishnu	Pramod... I don't know how you were born, man. But generally a child begins to grow inside a woman... *(Pramod glares at him)*
Mona	You don't know my Papa... his temper... and especially nowadays... he's like *hazaar* tense...
Pramod	*Tense...*? What about...?
Mona	The elections are around the corner...
Nick	*Elections*??
Mona	The assembly elections. All these awful rumours have started... nasty, unfair rumours... the media is out to screw my Papa.
Pramod	*Woah, woah*... elections... rumours, what are you talking about, Mona?
Vishnu	*Uh*... Mona... who exactly is your old man...? I'll bet he's either a drug lord or a gang lord?
Mona	He's a big politician...
Vishnu	See, I was right.
Mona	He's an MLA... he's standing as an Independent candidate from Satara.
Vishnu	Terrific. What's his name?
Mona	Sanjay Mansekar
Nick	Oh, the cricket commentator?
Vishnu	That's Sanjay Manjrekar, Einstein.
Pramod	Sanjay Mansekar...? I've heard the name... He's caught up in some scandal...?

Mona	They're accusing my Papa of kidnapping a journalist…
Pramod	(*blown*) The Rajshri Gholap case… shit, it's all over the papers.
Vishnu	This is a truly action packed morning… and the sun isn't even out yet.
Mona	My dad is innocent, okay…
Vishnu	Funny, I'm sure General Gaddafi felt the same way.
Mona	He has some very powerful enemies who want to bring him down.
Pramod	But Mona… your surname is Mehta… not Mansekar…
Mona	Yes… I kept my mother's maiden name… I don't want people to know who my father is… I want my own identity. I only use his name… sometimes.
Vishnu	When it is required, right?
Mona	Of course.
Vishnu	Of course… smart girl.
Mona	I want people to listen to me, okay?
Vishnu	Whatever…
Nick	Man, Khandu, this is s-s-s… serious shit… don't you know anything about the people you're screwing?
Pramod	Mona… why didn't you tell me all this earlier…?
Mona	Tell you what?

Pramod	That you're not just any ordinary chick I met at a bar. That you have a politician father who will nail my ass. And that you're carrying a baby that may or may not be mine. Why didn't you tell me all this earlier?
Mona	*(beat)* You never asked…
Vishnu	*(laughs)* Woah… deadly *line… 'you never asked'*
Pramod	…You think this is funny, Vishnu?
Vishnu	No… I don't. But I hide behind jokes. That's my way of relieving tension. Nicky stammers, you lie… I joke. You should try it sometime. It's less harmful than lying.
Mona	So you see, Prammy… you have a lot of thinking to do… choices, dude, choices.

(Another vomiting attack, Mona rushes to the toilet)

Vishnu	*(sings)* Pretty Woman… *walking down the street… pretty women…*
Nick	*(To Pramod, pushes him)* What the f-f-fuck have you got us involved in??
Pramod	Shut up *ya*…!! Anyway, this is my problem… why are you getting so antsy…
Nick	*Ya* right, your problem…!!! When this politician *goonda* sends his guys to nail your ass… we're all going to be here too… a victim of your crossfire…
Vishnu	*'Victim of your cross fire'?*
Pramod	Can you see why I wanted to get her out of here?

Vishnu	Get her out?? I think we need to get you far out of here, buddy, to maybe… Mars… or Saturn.
Nick	Pramod, man, she's a hot number…
Vishnu	Hot potato.
Nick	*What*??
Vishnu	The term is '*hot potato*' not '*hot number*'…
Nick	M-M-Man, Vishnu, why are you giving me English lessons just now??
Vishnu	So, is there a certain thrill screwing a politician's daughter…?
Nick	Like tasting forbidden fruit, I'll bet?
Vishnu	On a serious note, what is your immediate POA, Mr. K…? No rush… accuracy is important.
Pramod	I don't know…
Nick	What if her father does f-f-finds out about the accident…?
Pramod	He'll bugger us. He can't afford another scandal… even if it is his own daughter involved…
Vishnu	Then we do have to go the cops… tell them everything.
Pramod	What do we tell them? That I was bonking Mansekar's daughter in the back seat of a Mitsubishi Lancer, when my friend was killed, and she's pregnant. How's that gonna look?
Vishnu	Pretty bad, if you ask me…

Nick	Forbidden fruit, it seems. *(Pramod glares at him)*
Pramod	Look, guys, Mona's Dad is this big politician *Dada* from the area... he'll have all the cops in his pocket ... I don't want to spend my old age in a four foot by four foot cell.
Vishnu	Khandu, think clearly... this is a devil and deep blue sea situation. Panvel cops versus Papa's goondas.

(Mona emerges from bathroom, she is in some pain, holding her stomach)

Pramod	Mona...
Mona	Prammy, I need a doctor...
Nick	Oh. That was q-q-quick...
Pramod	A doctor...?
Mona	Prammy, I've got very bad cramps...
Nick	You were fine this morning... in the car...
Mona	I'm not fine now... okay! Pramod... my stomach is really hurting.
Pramod	Where will we find a doctor at this time?
Mona	Prammy, let's just get out of this shit.
Pramod	What, *now*??
Mona	Yes, we can go to a place where no one knows us.
Pramod	*Pagal hai kya?*
Mona	What's the problem, Prammy... my stomach is really hurting...

Pramod   I can't, Mona.

Mona   Why not?

Pramod   Mona… I can't…

Nick   *(cuts through, loud) He's married*!! *(quieter)* He's married.

Mona   *(stunned pause) You're what…?* *(to the others)* He's what… Vishnu… is this true?

Vishnu   Maybe…

Mona   What d'you mean, maybe?

Vishnu   *Uh…* it depends…

Mona   On what?

Vishnu   On what you will do to him if he is…

Mona   Cut his balls off…

Vishnu   Just give me an hour… I'll speak to the Registrar of Marriages…

Mona   *(very sharp)* This is not a joke… Vishnu!!

Vishnu   *(immediate)* Yes, Maam. She's fair skinned… wheat complexioned actually. She's five foot four. Her name is Seema. It used to be Anuradha. But now it's Seema. And they've been man and wife for 12 whole years.

Mona   *(as the reality sinks in)* Pramod, you bastard… .I've put up with your crap for six months… seedy bloody bars… dirty two star hotels… darkened movie halls… and this is my give back present !!

Pramod   Mona…

Mona	Don't Mona me, you *chuth! (guttural, almost animal growl)* Do you know who I *am*…?
Vishnu	Sanjay Mansekar's only daughter…?
Mona	*(she moves to Pramod and sits deliberately on his lap)* Yes… and you better believe it… I am Sanjay Mansekar's only daughter. *(beat)* You know what I'm going to do. I'm going to abort this child. Then I will tell my Papa, you made me kill his only grandchild.. And you know what he's going to do… he will make sure every cop, in every district, in every *taluka* in Maharashtra, will be after you. And then try going back to your wife… if she's still there when you go home… *(she kisses him deliberately) Bechara Baal. (she exits, a car passes on the highway)*
Vishnu	*Oooo,* man… this chick reminds me of Lara Croft in a bad mood…
Nick	I feel various parts of my anatomy getting cold. *(hysterical) Oh boy, we're s-s-screwed… we're* fucking *screwed…*
Vishnu	Nicholas… just zip it, okay? No panic stations right now. Go occupy yourself… go read a Thesaurus… play some carrom with yourself… better still just go down and get your car repaired… we need to get out of here soon.
Nick	You sure you guys will be okay… you don't need my help?
Vishnu	It will be horrendously difficult without you, but we'll manage. *Ciao…*

(Nicky exits obediently, Pramod and Vishnu are alone, beat, the mood quietens)

Vishnu   Think she'll spill the beans to her old man?

Pramod   50-50.

Vishnu   Why 50-50?

Pramod   She may not because it implicates her too. Plus she's terrified of the old man.

Vishnu   Conversely, she might tell him just to get back at you… right?

Pramod   *Ya.*

Vishnu   What are you going to do, Pramod?

Pramod   About what…?

Vishnu   About World Peace… about the Al Qaeda. Obviously about this babe. You've knocked her up, man. And she's a kid… cradle snatcher.

Pramod   I swear I thought she was taking precautions.

Vishnu   It's too late for that. Why weren't *you* protected?

Pramod   Who has the time to reach for one's wallet.

Vishnu   Pramod… no judgement… but you are married you know…

Pramod   Arranged marriages suck, man. Vishnu, it's like Seema is married to my mom. There's just no chemistry… no excitement between us.

Vishnu   *Chemistry? (indicating Mona)* And that's what you have with Miss Sulphuric Acid?

Pramod	Vish... it was really great initially. She really understood me...
Vishnu	She's cool that you're a professional thief...?
Pramod	I'm not a thief...!!
Vishnu	Forgive me... the conversion of white money into black is now a Fortune 500 business...?
Pramod	Vish, you wouldn't understand... you have that typical 9 to 5 Multinational mindset.
Vishnu	You gamble with other people's money...
Pramod	So do you...
Vishnu	*Ha ha ha...* Khandu... you really are the older brother I never had and I love you, but don't ever compare yourself with me...
Pramod	*Kyon?* How are we different... tell me...?
Vishnu	Pramod, man, comparisons are odious, and I don't judge you... but you're a scam artist... I'm not. I am in the Merger Acquisition business. You're in the rip-off business...
Pramod	At least I'm my own boss, Vishnu.
Vishnu	*Own boss*?! You've been running since you were 15, *man*! Hiding like a rat in the shadows... breathing back alley sewer air!
Pramod	*Acha*? I don't take shit from a Board, just so I can keep my company flat. I don't get a cheque every month with a salary deducted at source. I give the fucking government what I feel like, when I feel like...

Vishnu	Is that right? The last time you gave the government anything, Narasimha Rao was Prime Minister. *(pause)* My friend, it's going to catch up with you some day.
Pramod	Maybe… maybe. But it's already caught up with you, buddy… I'm still a free man.
Vishnu	Free, *huh*? I wouldn't call a man who pisses away his dosh at the racetrack, a free man…
Pramod	Look… I don't gamble, okay. I place very safe bets.
Vishnu	I ain't Freud, bro… but the first step in kicking any addiction, is to first accept you have it.
Pramod	Is that how you kicked your coke habit?
Vishnu	Woah, nasty… that is so way below the belt…
Pramod	I'm not the only one with the mindfucks, Vish.
Vishnu	Coke isn't a mind fuck, Pramod. Gambling is a mind fuck. Whips and chains are a mind fuck. Soya biscuits are a mind fuck. *Coke*? Coke is the real thing. Oh man… coke is Apollo 13 stuff. It defies gravity. You're like Mohammed of fucking Ghazni. Nothing… nobody can touch you. Institutions, companies falling at your feet. The world hanging onto your every offer. You wanna buy, buy. Offer open till stocks last. And you're the one who owns the stocks.
Pramod	Yeah… till you're caught sniffing the stuff in your office loo, *huh*?
Vishnu	*(smiles ruefully)* Yeah… a significant dip in my career curve… I gotta admit.

Pramod   Bad scene, *huh*?

Vishnu   Spend most of my life '*doing the right thing*'. The one time I waver, I get hung. Man, Pramod, you dance with the law, everyday, and you rock.

Pramod   Are you clean now?

Vishnu   *Ya.* Painfully. I miss the line, though.

Pramod   The *line*?

Vishnu   (*indicates sniffing*) Khandu, man. The line. What I don't miss however are the nightmares... and the paranoia... and the mood swings... and the cold shivers... and the time when I could just kill for 5 milligrams of fucking white powder. But, hey, I'm alive, *right*?

Pramod   Where did that come from?

Vishnu   I don't know... from an hour ago. Babu's death is hitting me now. Nicky's right... we let the big man down... very badly.

Pramod   How?

Vishnu   We just sat in the car, Khandu... I just froze.

Pramod   We would all have been killed...

Vishnu   Pramod... this is me and you, man... not the cops... not the courts... get real... we valued our lives more than his. It could have been you dead on that highway. (*beat*) We were just too chicken to help. Judo lessons... thrice a week. But come crunch time, I just blew it.

Pramod   Don't be so hard on yourself, *okay...*?

Vishnu	*Hard…* Hard on myself? You're kidding, right? *(small beat)* I'm saying to myself '*Get off your butt, fight this incredible injustice*'. But my mind and body were in perfect disharmony. I couldn't move. Feet tied with rocks. Man, twenty years of friendship gone in a pool of blood. *(to Pramod)* You don't feel anything…? No guilt… no sense of loss?
Pramod	Of course… but there's no time to mourn just now… Grief will slow us down.
Vishnu	Wow!! Amazing how you can time table your emotions… *(takes out imaginary diary)* Okay… let me check my diary… 9 am… our hour set aside for Happiness. 10 am… I have an appointment with Depression… oh, no, no time just now. I think I'll slot it for later. Let's see… I will push it down to 6 pm. Oh shit that might clash with Aggression hour… how do I table this, I'm just too busy to feel anything?!!!
Pramod	Okay… okay… you've made your point. Look, I find it tough to express my emotions. *Madu* boys are conditioned from an early age never to show their vulnerability.
Vishnu	*Why*, because the Stock Market might crash?

(They both smile, beat. Nick screaming offstage)

Nick	*(Offstage) Hey you… you waiter guy… Sakharam…*
Pramod	*Hey Bhagwan… yeh kahan se aaaya.*
Vishnu	Nick is becoming like piles… an unending pain in the ass.

Pramod	How did he know we were going to Lonavala?
Vishnu	The guy's lonely… obviously time hangs heavy with him… dude calls me six times a day…
Pramod	But why did you have to tell him we were going??
Vishnu	I feel sorry for him. Poor little rich boy.
Pramod	Why?
Vishnu	I don't know, everything. His stammer… no Dad, his childhood, man. He had a very weird house… don't you remember?
Pramod	No man, I was too busy ogling at his Mom… staring at her… uh… *(indicates breasts)*
Vishnu	*Ya…* her beautiful eyes… I get it. According to me, the slutty Mrs. Thomas was a major part of the problem…
Pramod	She used to kiss him on the lips, but what else?
Vishnu	Man, Pramod, she was bonking half of Worli's hot blooded males. Nick would come home from school. '*Hi Mom, I'm back'*… She'd emerge from the bedroom buttoning up her blouse… *(imitates Nick's Mom)* '*Nicky, meet uh Mr. Das… he's selling me Life Insurance.'* I'll never forget Nicky telling me, *(imitates Nicky)* '*Man, it was f-f-f-fucking hilarious, this guy coming out of my parents room, zipping up his fly with one hand and holding up a policy in the other'*. I'm surprised he got away with only a stammer.

(Nick bursts into the room, a mental mess)

Nick	Man… f-f-f-fuck… problem… problem. *(Pramod & Vishnu exchange looks and smile wryly)* Why are you guys laughing. I can't f-f-f-fix the car… we're rogered…
Pramod	Why not?
Nick	The fan belt has gone… there's some blessed leakage… we must have hit something when we stopped. And some b-b-b…
Vishnu	*(helping Nick)* Bloke…? Bugger…? *(Nick points at Pramod)* Aaah… *Bastard*?
Nick	*Ya*, bastard… has punctured all four tyres.
Vishnu	Fabulous run of luck.
Nick	By the way, there's no one at this hotel… except us, the porn stars next door and the two characters downstairs from *DARNA MANA HAI*.
Pramod	How did Mona leave…?
Nick	I don't know… *(suddenly his phone rings)* Hello… hello… *(network bad)* Hello… who… oh hello Diana …*(Pramod, Vishnu's ears perk up, Nick embarrassed)*
Pramod	How did you get a signal, *ya*…?
Nick	Yes… *uh*… no… tomorrow… *ya*… no we might have to cancel… *ya*… I won't be back… who… oh the others… *uh*… c-c-c… can you call them… Maria… Giselle… Sameera… thanks. God bless you too *(hangs up phone and looks at them sheepishly)*
Vishnu	*Uh*… big date, *huh*, stud…?
Nick	Not a date…

Vishnu   Dude, why you suddenly blushing?

Nick   I'm not blushing.

Vishnu   Nicholas Thomas, you look like a sun burnt hippie. Spill it, buddy

Nick   *(beat)* Okay, I conduct a d-d-d-dance class

Pramod   *What?*!! What kind of dance?

Vishnu   Not ballet, I hope… (*Both Pramod and Vishnu laugh*)

Nick   No… no… ya… not bloody ballet *(beat)* S-S-S-Salsa

Pramod   *What*…?!

Vishnu   You teach Salsa…???

Nick   Yup… to older ladies in the Church.

Vishnu   Man, you think you know a guy. (*asks Nick to come close, then grabs his leg, laughing*) You don't also wear women's underwear, *right*?

Nick   Just f-f-f-fuck off.

(*All three are laughing uproariously. Suddenly the waiter enters, to their total surprise, sits down before they can speak*)

Waiter   *Jaani mamla, bahut gambheer hai. Woh ladki* Mansekar *seth cha mulgi hai…*

Nick   *Tumko*… how do you know?

Waiter   *Woh humko sab kuch saangeethla. Abhi tera teeno ka* ticket… *sampla… khallas.*

Nick   What the f-f-f-fuck's he talking about??

Waiter	*Phakth… phakth naahi… tum (points at Pramod) tumne mulgi ko maara… thapad diya… Maatharya*
Pramod	What crap… the babe is lying… I never touched her.
Vishnu	A woman scorned, buddy… this waiter dude won't believe you…
Pramod	Mona must have slapped herself a couple of times
Waiter	*Pone aala…*
Pramod	*Kiska* phone…?
Waiter	*Dhondu cha.*
Nick	Who the f-f-fuck is Dhondu…?
Waiter	Mansekar *seth cha dipti… majha dost (the three exchange quick looks)*
Pramod	Oh man, she called her Dad…
Vishnu	Who in turn called his chief henchman…
Pramod	*Kya bola?*
Waiter	*Tumara yahan se jaana* allowed *nahin aahe.*
Nick	What's he saying… why can't we leave?
Pramod	*Kaun rokega humko?*
Waiter	*Mee. Sakharam.* Dhondu *aur unka aadmi idhar aa raha hai. Humko bola tumko rukaneko. Yeh mera* order *hai.*
Pramod	*Tum humko kaisa rukaega?*
Nick	This bugger's getting on my t-t-t-tits… the three of us can get him, *ya*
Vishnu	No, I think the old man has something up his sleeve.

Waiter	*Tum log kidhar jayega… hey mala saanga. (beat) Gaadi kharaab… chaaron* tyre *(takes a drag of his beedi)… phusssss…*
Nick	*Tumne* tyre… he d-d-d-d-d…
Vishnu	*Ya…* he deflated the tyres…
Waiter	*Haan, mee…* Sakharam.
Pramod	I think he's bullshitting about these rowdies heading here. What d'you think, Vish?
Vishnu	Old Daddyo will want to cover up *beti's* wayward behavior. He has enough hassles as it is… he'll want to crush us.
Nick	How do we leave, man… how do we get back to Bombay…?
Waiter	No going Mumbai, *Bhau.*
Pramod	*Kyon*??
Waiter	*Nai… heych* area *madhi bandh…*
Pramod	What do you mean, *bandh*?
Waiter	*Yeh* area *mein poora bandh…* total. *Tumhara* Mumbai *bandh, hamara* Panvel *bandh… (takes out newspaper, hands it to them) Padho… padho. Tum kidhar nahin jayega.* Hotal Moonlight *mein* lock up.
Nick	*(looking at newspaper)* It's in Hindi…
Pramod	Marathi. *(to Vishnu)* We're stuck…
Vishnu	C'mon guys, Don Corleone here wants to play chess… so let's play…

Pramod   *Kya chahiye tumko?*

Waiter   *Kya chahiye... kya chahiye. (beat) Maaphi. (points at Nick) Woh humse maaphi lega... aata...* now!

(Pramod and Vishnu simultaneously speak)

Pramod   *Kyon?*

Vishnu   What...?

Waiter   *Usne humko* insult *kiya... maajha aai cha badnaam kiya... (imitates Nicky)* 'Your *aai, snan* bathing'... *(angry)* Sorry *bolo, tujha aila.*

Pramod   *(quietly to Vishnu)* What's this about?

Vishnu   This is pound of flesh time. He's toying with us. *(thinking quickly)* Nicky apologize...

Nick   Why the f-f-f...

Pramod   Just do it... so we can move to stage two.

Nick   What's wrong with you guys... he's insulted us... he's messing with us... and I have to apologize.

Vishnu   Bite your tongue, Nicky... you lose nothing except some valuable self-respect... but what the hell.

Nick   *(great difficulty)* Sorry...

Waiter   *(cups ear) Kai...? Maine suna nahin... zor se saanga... Bola bola.*

Nick   *(louder)* SORRY... *(fights instinct to insult)*

Waiter   *(beat, then unexpectedly) Nahin...* sorry *nahin chalnaar...*

Nick   What the f-f-f-f-?

Vishnu	I thought as much…
Waiter	*(points to his feet) Mere pao ko chuo…*
Nick	What's the b-b-b-bugger saying??
Pramod	He wants you to touch his feet…
Nick	W-w-w-why??
Vishnu	Maybe he wants you to give him a pedicure.
Waiter	*Chala chala Bhau…* time *nahin hai mala*
Vishnu	Khandu…
Pramod	Yup…
Vishnu	Let me negotiate with this guy…
Pramod	Why?
Vishnu	Pramod… I do this for a living… trust me…
Pramod	Vish, let's just pay the bugger and be done with it.
Vishnu	No way, man… let's at least give this guy a run for his money.
Pramod	I hope you're right.
Vishnu	Me too. *(to waiter)* So Dhondu *aa raha hai kya… kabhi?*
Waiter	*Abhi… abhi… woh* Panvel *main hai…* Dhondu Panvel *ka dada hai…*
Vishnu	*(very fast, soft, just enough for waiter to hear) Tu tyacha chela aahe?*
Waiter	*Kya??*
Vishnu	*Tu tyacha manoos aahe?*

Waiter	*(defensive) Main apna aadmi hai...*
Vishnu	*Kitna paisa diya tumko...?*
Waiter	*Kaun,* Dhondu?
Vishnu	Dhondu... *nahin.* Mansekar...
Waiter	*(corrects him) Mansekar seth!!!*
Vishnu	*Tu* Mansekar *ko mila hai, na?*
Waiter	*Haan, haan, bahuth baar...*
Vishnu	*Uhm... woh kitna paisa deta hai tumko?*
Waiter	*Uhm...*
Vishnu	Mansekar *tumko paisa deta hai, na?*
Waiter	*Haan haan, paisa deto mala... khub deto*
Vishnu	*Kitna??*
Waiter	*Main kyon bolu tula?*
Vishnu	*Kitna...? Bees... tees... aadha taka... ek taka?*
Waiter	*Ek taka...*
Vishnu	*Bas... sirf ek taka. (laughs mockingly) Tumko ullu bana diya... tum Panvel se hai, na? Iske liye... Woh tumko Panvel ka rate de raha hai... tsk... tsk... bechara Sakharam... (laughs at him, he is humiliated)*
Pramod	*Tumko bilkul izzat nahin deta hai*
Waiter	*Eh... eh... bak bak math kara... woh humko bahuth izzat deta hai!!!*
Vishnu	*(dismissing him)* Please *chalo... niklo yahan se... phuto...*

Waiter	*Kya*?? *Bahuth charbee dikhatha hai... dekho main* warning *deta hai tula... theek se soch lo.*
Vishnu	*Soch liya.* No boss... *tum hamare liye...* useless... *Hum* Dhondu *se baat karega.*
Waiter	Dhondu *se baath karega...*?? *Mee boltho tula...* Dhondu *bahuth danger aadmi hai. Woh tumse nahin baath karega... sirf mere saath. (they are silent, go about their business, as if the waiter isn't in the room. The waiter ponders, suddenly) Tum teeno ke liye* discount. *Dus hazaar...*
Vishnu	*(mock surprise)Tum kuch bola?*
Waiter	*Hum bola... dus hazaar... humko dus hazaar do*
Vishnu	*Nahin...* discussion *bandh*
Waiter	*Dus hazaar, bahut kum aahe*
Nick	*(under his breath)* Vishnu... let's do it... man...
Vishnu	*(under his breath)* Nick... shut up... *(to waiter) Nahin boss.*
Waiter	*Eh... yeh* Sakharam *ka ilaka hai...*
Pramod	*Nahin boss... yeh* Mansekar *ka illaka hai...*
Waiter	*Mansekar ka illaka... huh... mera galti ho gaya...??? (he takes out a knife, cuts Pramod who recoils) Accha,* offer *sampla. Poora paisa nikalo. Tum log samajtha nahin. Main bola dus hazaar... tum log hushiari dikhata hai. Abhi pachthayega... poora paisa nikalo, chal !!! (they are forced to take out all their money)Chalo idhar rakho... chala chala... hey Sunny... Romeo...*

Pramod	Yes… I think so. What happened to your negotiation skills, Vish.
Vishnu	You could say a weapon of mass destruction interfered.
Waiter	*Hum bola… tum suna nahin… Abhi* Dhondu *aayega… (waiter exits singing)*
Nick	Are you c-c-c-crazy? We should have paid the guy earlier… now we have no money… what do we do?
Vishnu	Should I call him back… tell him that you want to kiss his feet…?
Nick	But those guys are coming for us… you don't understand?
Vishnu	Nicky, I'm fast tiring of your attitude. Childhood was several years ago. Get positive, man.
Pramod	Why didn't you want to pay?
Vishnu	I spend my days negotiating with sharks far sharper than this idiot… he would've taken our money and double crossed us anyway… I had to provide some resistance.
Pramod	Think this Dhondu guy is on his way…?
Vishnu	Yup, I'm almost certain. Sequence of events – Mona squealed to her Dad. Dad summoned Dhondu to come here and deal with us. Simple. The waiter just wants a piece of the action.
Pramod	What d'you wanna do…?
Vishnu	We need to find a way to get out of here… now.
Nick	And Babu…?

Pramod   What about him…?

Nick   Babu is lying… wounded… or d-d-d-dead somewhere on the highway, we don't know. We're just going to leave him?

Pramod   Look if we don't split… it's going to be four bodies on that highway.

Nick   What are we going to tell his Mom… *huh*… that her son was s-s-s-stabbed by some *goondas*… that we did nothing to help… and we just left him to his fate…

Vishnu   Nicky… I know how you feel… man, I feel as terrible but…

Nick   How I feel… how I feel…? How do you feel… *huh*… how do you guys feel? He was our friend. Pramod, when Babu, you and I first met… we had no f-f-fucking hair on our upper lip… our b-b-bloody voices hadn't cracked yet. Does that mean nothing…?

Pramod   Nicky…

Nick   Don't 'Nicky' me… you guys want to get back to Bombay, right… tell me… if you guys wanna go… *ciao*. Here's my d-d-d-deal, I'm staying…

Vishnu   Run that by me again…?

Nick   I'm staying. I'm not coming with you guys.

Vishnu   Your chances of survival are as slim as an anorexic model, bud… this is unfamiliar terrain for you.

Nick   Look… I'm not saying I'm not scared. God knows, I'm even more t-t-t-terrified to know what happened

to Babu. But I've got to do this... for myself... for
Babu. Otherwise, it will haunt me forever.

Pramod   *Uh*... what exactly are you going to do?

Nick   I have a plan...

Vishnu   Want to give us a brief synopsis?

Nick   I'm going to the cops...

Vishnu   That's not a synopsis. That's a sad ending.

Pramod   Nicky... we've been through this before...

Nick   I will tell them everything that happened. Whatever
the consequences.

Pramod   Whatever the consequences? *Huh?*

Nick   *Ya.*

Pramod   Whatever they do to you, *huh?*

Nick   *Ya.*

(Atmosphere changes. Like a police station, Pramod like an interrogator)

Pramod   You and Babu did get out of the car?

Nick   *Huh...??!*

Pramod   Why did you stop the car?

Nick   There was something lying across the road... it looked
like a body.

Pramod   So why did you get out of the car?

Nick   You asked Babu to check out what was on the road...
I... went with him.

Pramod   What was on the road?

Nick	We couldn't tell at first. When we got close... we realized it was a big sack... of rice... of grain... or something... made to look like a body.
Pramod	So then what did you do?
Nick	*(unfocussed)* We decided to leave it... started to come back to the car.
Pramod	What happened next...?
Nick	*Huh*?
Pramod	What happened next?
Nick	S-s-s-suddenly... suddenly... *(finds it hard to go on)*
Pramod	Suddenly what?!!!
Nick	*(remembers the incident)* It was a trap... there were these guys, man...
Pramod	What guys???
Nick	A gang of guys... with knives... swords... they came out of nowhere... we d-d-d-didn't see them coming.
Pramod	Why not?
Nick	It was drizzling... it was dark... we couldn't see anything... they were on us...
Pramod	What did they do?
Nick	They... *uh*...
Pramod	*(cuts him) What did they do?*
Nick	They attacked Babu... we had no t-t-t-time to react... they were hitting him... I shouted to Babu... *'lets run'*...
Pramod	So did you run... *did you*...?

Nick	We tried… I managed… to get away, to get to the car. Why are you asking me all these…???
Pramod	*(cuts him)* What happened to Babu…?
Nick	*(backing into wall)* I thought he was following. I turned to look. Babu… *uh*… Babu had slipped… they were on him… I turned around… He was f-f-f-fucking reaching out to me… begging me to come back… blood on his hands… but I didn't… *we* didn't… we drove off… we left him to die… f-f-f-fuck… f-f-f-fuck…!!! *(breaks down)* Why are you doing this…?
Pramod	*(very close to him)* Okay… now imagine all these identical questions coming at you… except instead of me, there is this *paan* chewing cop…
Vishnu	Okay, Khandelwal, cut the Hitler routine… just back up a second, Nicky… am I hearing things… but did you say they were attacking Babu?
Nick	*Ya*…
Vishnu	They weren't attacking you too…?
Nick	No they weren't… *(realization strikes)* Oh shit…!!!
Pramod	*Huh*?? What are you getting at??
Nick	They were only t-t-t-targeting Babu.
Vishnu	Let me get this straight… they didn't hurt you?
Nick	*(shows arms, chest)* Just look, I have no c-c-c-cuts and bruises. Sure, they pushed and shoved me… but more to get me out of the way. They were definitely after Babu.
Vishnu	How did you get away then?

Nick	I kneed the guy in the balls. And ran. That's how I got away so easily, nobody chased me… they were too busy f-f-f-finishing off Babu.
Pramod	But I thought he slipped.
Nick	No, he was badly injured… they beat him repeatedly… he fell…
Pramod	But why didn't you think of this earlier?
Nick	I don't know, man… it didn't hit me then… I was so g-g-g-guilty about leaving Babu… I wasn't thinking clearly. But I am sure now.

(a beat as they reassess the situation)

Vishnu	So what are we saying here, guys…?
Nick	That this wasn't an… an… a-c-c-c…
Vishnu	An accident…
Pramod	How can that be… it's impossible… it's crazy.
Nick	But why would they only attack Babu… why not me??
Pramod	Somehow it doesn't fit…
Nick	What doesn't f-f-fit???
Pramod	Why would somebody want to attack us… attack Babu… in the middle of the highway, at 5 in the morning…
Vishnu	More importantly, how would they know we'd be there… at that exact point… at that exact time? *(beat)* Unless…
Pramod	Unless, what?

Vishnu	Unless… one of us is involved…
Nick	What the f-f-f-fuck are you talking about…?
Vishnu	Think about it… any one of us could have told them…
Nick	You're insane… Why in heaven's name would any of us want B-B-B-Babu dead… our own gentle Big Moose?
Pramod	Chill Nicky… Vishnu is kidding. Did he have any enemies?
Vishnu	The bloke was just a fitness instructor for crying out aloud…
Pramod	Personal training is a big business today…
Nick	How was he doing for money?
Vishnu	*(a beat)* Badly.
Nick	How do you know?
Vishnu	He told me. Was very vague about the details… but I sensed he was in deep shit.
Nick	What does that mean…?
Vishnu	He lived way beyond his means…
Pramod	So what's new?
Vishnu	Meaning?
Pramod	C'mon, Babu was always broke. Right from when we were kids. He was always borrowing from Vish and me…
Nick	Vish?
Vishnu	Yes… he did borrow the occasional buck…

Pramod	*(sudden anger)* Occasional buck, my ass. The bugger would come *pao padaoing* all the time and never return the dosh.
Vishnu	Old habits die hard, I suppose.
Pramod	Yeah… he probably owed me lakhs.
Vishnu	Man, you have issues with Babu. Hadn't realized you were so angry.
Pramod	I'm not angry. Bugger just took and took… never returning… always lame bloody excuses…
Vishnu	Pramod… man… I'm caught in a minor time warp. Why is there an air of the present in your tone? Do you know something I don't…?
Pramod	Just get off my back, okay?
Vishnu	Pramod… I'm not on it yet. What the fuck is going on… did Babu speak to you? *(Pramod is fighting with himself)* You know bud… there's no way you'd pass a lie detector test, right now… look at your face. Pramod, if you know something… now's a good time to reveal… *(Pramod is unable to speak. His mind is racing, he has turned away)* Pramod… what's up, man… you look like you've seen a ghost…

(Vishnu is staring at Pramod, who is at a loss for words. A beat. Then Pramod looks up at Vishnu. He can't look directly into his eyes. Then he does. There is a moment when the two friends are face to face, looking into each other's eyes. Vishnu sees a flicker)

| Nick | Look, guys… I'm a simple f-f-f-fucking Brahmin boy from the coast… all these looks you guys are exchanging are f-f-frightening the shit out of me… what's going on? |

Vishnu (*still looking at Pramod, circumspectly*) Uh… Nicky… I don't know what's going on… though I do have a sinking feeling that the next few minutes are going to be crucial for all of us. (*softly to Pramod*) Pramod… I have to admit I share Nick's fear… and your abject silence isn't helping much either.

Pramod Babu came to me… last year, okay. He was in deep financial shit. Asked me, for, you know a contact. I… uh… know someone, *ya*. The problem is the guy made me stand guarantor. Which I did, like a bloody fool. Babu screwed up. C'mon, guys, you know Babu. *'I'm sorry, ya, I can't pay now, ya… next month, Naki'.* So the bastard came after me. They came to the house, man. Told Seema they would break my knees. (*beat, looks at them, they are staring at him*) Look it wasn't meant to be like this…

Vishnu Maybe it's a coke withdrawal thing… but you need to slow down, Pramod. What '*wasn't meant to be like this…*'?

Pramod He wanted to teach Babu a lesson… give him a serious warning. So they asked me to bring him to an appointed place.

Vishnu Why did they choose the highway?

Pramod I suggested that…

Vishnu Why?

Pramod It's easy to trace someone in Bombay…

Vishnu Wow… what foresight… lead your best friend to a lonely highway… get away scot free…

Pramod   It's not like that, Vishnu.

Vishnu   *Really*!! Tell me how it is. It's all so fascinatingly clear to me now, Khandelwal. Hear me out. Let me walk you through this. Scenario. Your hoodlums think, Babu is going to be easy meat. So they puncture his body like a Bridgestone fucking tyre. Blood spurting out of him, like a tasteless water fountain. But you're not sure he's dead, right? You're not sure that the burly lad you played seven tiles and tennis ball cricket with, is dead. You've got to check it out. You creep back, on all fours, like the slimy feline that you are. And Babu lives. So you complete the job that your moneylender started.

Pramod   Vishnu, that's not true, man. I would never hurt Babu. You have to believe me. He said he would only talk to Babu. Threaten him... when they started to attack him... I... I... they went back on their word. Vishnu... Vish... you have to believe me.

Vishnu   Belief is dead, man. You left belief, back there on that highway, dying. You stabbed belief squarely in the back, without a blink.

Pramod   Vish...

Vishnu   Shut up... shut up, right now. There cannot be dialogue between us anymore. Not a word, not a syllable. There is no you and I ever again, Pramod Khandelwal. We are a closed chapter.

Pramod   Vish...

Vishnu   We are a closed chapter.

(The waiter enters)

Waiter   *Chalo, chalo,* Dhondu *aa gaya… neeche chalo… chal phatafat.*

Vishnu   *(low, ominous to waiter)* I will warn you only once. We need our privacy. This is not a good time to interrupt. Please leave, immediately.

Waiter   *'Pleej leave…?' tujha aila… (He takes out a knife. In a flash, Vishnu in Judo mode, knocks the knife out of waiters' hands. Hits him hard in the chest. The waiter falls to the ground)*

Vishnu   *(gradually breaks his neck)* What are you gonna do? What are you gonna do that can possibly match what has happened here. How can you possibly make it worse. Huh… huh… *(beat, looks at Pramod)* You think you know a guy…

(Pramod goes upto waiter, takes his pulse, indicates waiter is dead. Silence. All three are quiet. Beat. The phone suddenly rings. No one responds for three rings. Then Pramod picks up receiver.)

Pramod   Hello… yes… *haan… haan.* Thank you. Hello… yes… Inspector… *haanji bolo… kya… haan… yes…* his name is Babu Dholakia… *haan… haan… kya… kya… my God! (Pramod is stunned)…* thank you… *haan…* thank you… *(He puts phone down. To them)* That was the cops. They're on their way here. Guys… it's about Babu. He's alive… he made it.

Vishnu   How did the cops know we're here…?

Nick   *(beat)* I told them…

BLACKOUT. END OF PLAY.

CRAB

Ram Ganesh Kamatham

About the Playwright

Writer–director Ram Ganesh Kamatham has created work for stage, film, radio, comics and video games. With a heady mix of dark humour and biting satire, his plays entertain, provoke and challenge audiences, confronting them with the problems of next-generation, young urban India.

A recipient of several awards and fellowships, including the 2011 Sultan Padamsee Award for playwriting, the Asif Currimbhoy Playwriting Fellowship and the Sarai-CSDS Independent Research Fellowship, Ram was the Executive Editor of *PT Notes*, the Prithvi Theatre's monthly newsletter from 2009 to 2011.

Some of his other work for the stage includes *Ultimate Kurukshetra* (2010), *Project S.T.R.I.P.* (2009), *Creeper* (2007), *Snakes & Ladders* (2005), *Dancing on Glass* (2004) and *Square Root of Minus One* (2002). His plays have been staged at festivals in India and abroad.

Crab

Crab was first performed at the Prithvi Theatre, Mumbai, India on January 17th, 2007, produced by Q Theatre Productions. The cast was as follows:

Jojo   Freishia Bomanbehram
Zamiel   Ankur Vikal
Priya   Devika Shahani Punjabi
Rocky   Ali Fazal

Director	Arghya Lahiri
Production Designers	Toral Shah, Pushan Kripalani, Arghya Lahiri
Lighting Designer	Arghya Lahiri
On Sound	Gautam Dhanu
Photography	Ameet Mallapur

Acknowledgements

'For Shvéta,
Cindu, Jacob, Swaroop, Amit, Quasar, Toral, Arghya
With love…

My thanks to:

Carl, Phyllida, Anupama, the amazing playwright gang; Faezeh, Shernaz, Kunaal, Nadir, Ayesha, Trishla, Zafar, Mukul – my actors in workshop; Devika, Ankur, Freishia, Ali – my incredible cast; Jersis, Sumit, Udit, Shakti, Jogaraj, Anil – the boys of Rope 3, Basic Mountaineering Course 195; the late C. Norbu; and Froggy…'

Playwright's Note

Crab occupies a curious place in the trajectory of my work. It seems to exist in a liminal space, like the characters in the play, and one can't really slot it into one set of preoccupations or another. *Crab* was written primarily as an unrelenting character study and I cite Harold Pinter's *Betrayal* as a conscious influence, and Patrick Marber's *Closer* as an unconscious influence – but these citations may be far too lofty and self-absorbed! The final play and performance however, had an incandescent intensity of its own and drew praise and criticism in equal measure. The austere aesthetic of the play was immediately recognized as noteworthy, but when this austerity resulted in the absence of any overt political indicators or familiar signposting, the play slipped into being perceived as a kind of young and muddled rumination on love and loss. The characters seemed very familiar, but we knew close to nothing about them. The plot was straightforward, but the timelines convoluted. The play seemed much too violent and corrosive to be a romantic comedy, but much too sentimental and meditative to be a political statement. The younger audiences found the characters extremely superficial and unlikeable, the older audiences were intrigued by this detailed depiction of the younger generation. These paradoxes are to be expected when one has a play titled *Crab* that insists on moving sideways with a fierce bony exterior, shielding a soft vulnerable interior!

Kirtana Kumar managed to abstract the play beautifully when she wrote in the *Indian Express:* 'Crab *has four characters, but one who matters. Zamiel. The existential heir of Meursault in his remorseless commitment to the truth and Gregor Samsa in his love that is deeper, more willing to take risks. In 2007, when achievement and success are defined by measly measures of employability, disposable income, group dynamics and other corporate-speak, the "alone-ness" of Zamiel is even more stark. And therefore quite darkly romantic...'*

Cast

JOJO, *mid twenties*
ZAMIEL, *mid twenties*
PRIYA, *late twenties*
ROCKY, *early twenties*

Setting

A ledge…

Note: The use of punctuation in this play is not meant to conform to the rules of grammar, but to suggest the method of delivery.

Act 1

I

(Moments after sunset
Zamiel leans on a ledge. Looks over. Ponders.
He flexes his fingers.
Jojo enters.)

Jojo   Gone?

Zamiel   Pretty.

Jojo   Gone.

Zamiel   Pretty but gone.

Jojo   Sorry I missed it.

Zamiel   There'll be another tomorrow.

Jojo   What's up? You ok?

Zamiel   Been thinking.

Jojo   Good stuff I hope.

Zamiel   Gimme kiss.

Jojo   Kiss.

Zamiel   Real kiss.

Jojo   I have to get back to work.

Zamiel   Back to your cell?

Jojo   You look tired.

Zamiel   I've been staring at the sun.

Jojo   See anything?

Zamiel   I'm exhausted.

Jojo   So am I.

Zamiel   I've been getting that creepy feeling again.
Something watching as I climb, waiting-looking over my shoulder... for the false move, the hold that gives way...

Jojo   Shall we go downstairs and have a hot cup of coffee?
I'll sign you in and we'll hang at the pantry for five minutes.

Zamiel   The guard asked me where I had been all these days.

Jojo   He's a guard.

Zamiel   We were laughing about the last time you and I were up here.

Jojo   I'm not amused.
Why are you talking about climbing?

Zamiel   What will you do when you go back?

Jojo   Work. I don't know.
I came here for you. And you're hardly here.
I don't know anymore.

(Zamiel sits on the ledge, looks over.)

Jojo   That's making me nervous.

Zamiel   I brought you here for a reason.

Jojo   Please get down from there.

Zamiel   I'm ok.

Jojo   I'm not.

Zamiel   Why what happened?

Jojo   I'm leaving!

Zamiel   The guard is cool.

Jojo   *(pause)* That's not what happened last time. I got into trouble.

Zamiel   I spoke to your security.

Jojo   I wish you wouldn't come to my work place and talk to my colleagues and get all pally with them alright.

Zamiel   Oh now a security guard is your colleague!

Jojo   Just don't screw things up for me.
             I want to work here a while in peace.

Zamiel   Guard on the eighth floor thinks highly of you.
             Says you're polite and on time.

Jojo   I don't care about his opinion.

Zamiel   He's from Kolar.
             Moved here when the gold fields collapsed.
             Came here with his family, where he could get a high-profile job.
             As a guard in this... IT giant.

Jojo	I've wasted my coffee break listening to stories about security guards.
Zamiel	Meeting me is a waste now.
Jojo	*(pause)* I love you.
Zamiel	I love you too.
Jojo	Please don't make it difficult for us.
Zamiel	Kiss?
Jojo	No. *(pause)* Kiss.
Zamiel	I brought you a present.
Jojo	No gifts!
Zamiel	Why?
Jojo	You're not supposed to buy me gifts anymore.
Zamiel	Didn't buy it.
Jojo	No gifts.
Zamiel	Too late.
Jojo	We agreed no gifts no phone calls, meet for lunch now and then. We're already meeting. Next you'll start_
Zamiel	You think by creating this distance you're changing things? *(pause)* Your nose is incredible when you get snappy.
Jojo	I'm leaving.
Zamiel	Just take it.
Jojo	No.

Zamiel   Pest.

(Zamiel reaches into a pocket and hands her a carabiner.
She ignores the gift, turns away.)

Zamiel   It saved my life. It's a carabiner.
              (pause) 18 Kilo Newton breaking strength, 8 Kilo
              Newton lateral stress, it's taken a beating.
              Has a hairline crack in it. I can't use it anymore.

Jojo   Interesting. I have no idea what you are saying.

Zamiel   Rock face in Ramnagaram. I slipped.
              Thirty foot drop.
              (points) That caught me.
              Took a bad rope burn. Happened last November.
              I was too scared to tell you then. Now... it doesn't
              matter.

Jojo   Why are you telling me now?

Zamiel   I don't care now.

Jojo   Great. Fuck off then.

Zamiel   Take it.

Jojo   Why?

Zamiel   It saved me. It's what held me. Like you.

(He gently places it in her hands and closes her fist around it.
She does not look at it.)

Jojo   You don't need saving.
              You don't need to do that stuff.
              Every time you go, I don't know if you're going to
              come back.

Why can't you just_

Zamiel   Are you going to ask me to stop climbing?

Jojo   No.
             You're free to do what you want.

Zamiel   I thought we wanted to be together.

Jojo   It takes effort.

Zamiel   Being with you was effortless.

Jojo   I'm not in the mood for this game. I'm starting my
             shift.

Zamiel   Bloodsucker.

Jojo   Not interested.

Zamiel   Goddess.

Jojo   Stop it.

Zamiel   Baby Jo.

Jojo   YOU CAN'T DO THIS!

Zamiel   I'm done. Done.

Jojo   Ok. Go.

Zamiel   I'm going.
             Away.
             For a… long while.
             North. High altitude.
             I can't be in the same city as you.

(Silence.)

Jojo   No.

Zamiel   No what?

Jojo   Nothing.

Zamiel   I'm out tomorrow morning.

Jojo   You're making this difficult.

Zamiel   Why?
It's something I have to do.

Jojo   No you don't.
You don't have to do anything.

Zamiel   I need to make my peace.

Jojo   You know I needn't really care.
I needn't loose sleep over worrying where you are.
Frankly I shouldn't give a shit.

Zamiel   Do you worry?

Jojo   Not anymore.
And I think that's the way we should leave it.

Zamiel   That's good then.
(pause) Wish me luck.

Jojo   Go stay climb do what ever you like.

Zamiel   I'd rather go with your blessing.

Jojo   Fuck you.

Zamiel   I want your leave.

Jojo   Leave.

Zamiel   You're being difficult.

Jojo   I'M being difficult?

You're making a mess of things. I can't deal with this.

(Silence.
Zamiel stands up on the ledge.
Walks.
Jojo begins to cry.)

Jojo	Go. Die. Fall and die.
Zamiel	Come here.
Jojo	No.
Zamiel	Come.
Jojo	NO.
Zamiel	Take my hand. Trust me.
Jojo	I'm not doing this.
Zamiel	We've done this.
Jojo	I'm not going back to this. I'm not.
	Do whatever you want.
	Find whatever the fuck you're looking for.
	I'm not going to be able to share it with you.
	You can play this game. I can't. I care too much.
Zamiel	It's lonely here.
Jojo	You need this more than I do.
	Keep it.

(She throws the carabiner up at Zamiel who catches it.
He squats, snapping it open and closed.)

II

(Jojo walks away, wiping her tears.
She rolls a joint, smokes it with relief.
She looks at a pair of bling joothis, slips into them.)

Jojo   I played with ants a lot.

There's a black ant called the *bachac* don't ask me why.

Inch long, big head. Got mandibles trap jaws whatever that are perfectly straight. Not curved. One eighty degrees wide open.

Take a stick, a bucket.

The *bachacs* build a complex network of passages underground.

Take the stick and poke through a section of the mud.

Use the stick and poke one in the mouth.

There's a nerve or hair or something between the mandibles that triggers them.

And 'TUP' they snap shut on the stick and the bachac goes flying backwards with the force of the attack. And another. TUP. TUP. TUP.

Use the bucket. Pour some water on the ant hill. It dissolves the mud walls.

They're upset now. Panic setting in as a vengeful goddess smashes their world with a wave of her hand.

Pour more water and stir the mud into a paste.

The complex subway system is now brown goo and the *bachac* colony is all covered in sticky mud drowning screaming mandibles clattering.

(pause) Look to your feet, sometimes they cut through the stick and bucket routine and see you for what you are.

Stir to get the right consistency. Leave to dry.

After about six minutes depending on the sun, cut the mud carefully and lift a section out like a slice of cake.

And there they are, frozen in time... sculpted-immortalized in terror...

A cross section of *bachac* society for you to keep.

III

(Rocky enters and slips a glove on her.
Jojo disinterestedly adjusts it. She's stoned.
Rocky watches, taps a wall with a bull's-eye on it.)

Rocky   Give it all you've got.
Everything.
Inhale then exhale with the punch. Sharp exhale.
GO!

(Silence. Jojo punches unenthusiastically, really lamely.)

Rocky   Ok ok ok. Not bad. Ten kgs.
That's really good.
(pause) If you're not feeling well I can take you home.

Jojo   No. I'm fine.

Rocky   You're fine?

Jojo   Peachy.

Rocky   You're well then?

Jojo   *(pause)* No, I'm going to drop dead now.

Rocky   I'll play for a bit?

Jojo   Please.

Rocky   *(pause)* Um… I need that.

(Jojo struggles to take the glove off. Rocky moves to help.)

Jojo   I'LL DO IT MYSELF!

Rocky   Fine cool rocking fine with me babes.

(Jojo tears the glove off, gives it to Rocky.
He casually puts on the glove.)

Rocky   There's a sale happening at Linking Road. Want to come along?
              I was planning on picking up some Caterpillars. We can have fun shopping?

Jojo   I'm a bit tired.

Rocky   The cool steel tipped ones.
              (pause) You want to pick up something for yourself?
              Or we could chill at KFC or something.

Jojo   I'd rather eat dog shit.

Rocky   *(pause)* The dogshit Zinger is decent.

Jojo   I don't eat genetically engineered chicken substitute kept alive by tubes that pump blood in and take shit out. They don't even have heads.

Rocky   Utter crap.
              How can they not have heads?

Jojo   For what? All YOU need is breasts and legs.

Rocky   What about wings?

Jojo   Ever wonder why the breasts are so fucking misshapen? It's like a huge blob of meat hacked off this hideous mutant creature_

Rocky   That is such utter rubbish.

This is just your food thing... You're still not eating properly are you?

Jojo   I'll eat what and when I want.

Rocky   You've been mind fucked by PETA fanatics.

Jojo   And you're ignorant.

Rocky   No. This is his dirty influence I suppose.
You should focus on work and important stuff.
How much of the stuff have you been smoking?
He's such a loser. And career! That's so critical right now.
Have you thought about what you want to do after you graduate?

Jojo   I'm going to Bangalore. He's there for the South Zone Qualifiers.
I'll figure it out.

Rocky   You're building your life around him now?

Jojo   You're ignorant.

Rocky   My knowledge of animal blobs is limited.

Jojo   Just animal blobs?

Rocky   So I'm stupid. I don't measure up?
Man what the fuck do you want?

Jojo   I'm spending time with you aren't I.

Rocky   You call this time.

Jojo   What is this then?

Rocky   I'm worried sick about you.

I thought this would be something fun we could do.
I never see you anymore.

Jojo   *(pause)* I'm not over stuff.

Rocky   I know. You need time_

Jojo   Look, don't make it sound_

Rocky   It's not easy.
But I want for you to move on.
And I want you_

Jojo   I'm not interested in what YOU want...

Rocky   You're really making this difficult.
(pause) Ten chits so far. We get some more we can get
a cool prize.

(He punches hard.)

Rocky   One fifty.

Jojo   Oh joyous day.

Rocky   If I punched someone who weighed a hundred kilos,
I'd take them off their feet with fifty kgs to spare!

Jojo   Too bad it's not your IQ.

Rocky   You're dense Rocky, you're ignorant Rocky, grow up,
get a life.
I'm not a genius. Fucking shoot me.

Jojo   Why waste a bullet.

Rocky   That chicken stuff is a hoax.

Jojo   If you're trying to_

Rocky	BUT I do know for a fact....
	That the real chickens, I looked it up, not your mutant blobs have their beaks chopped off. And they're drugged to make them fatter....
	And this is the funniest they get so fat and top heavy that their legs break because they can't take the weight and they sort of kick about in circles trying to get up. Like it's at a disco and it's doing the helicopter but it's a chicken with broken legs.
	(laughs) It's like hip hop. It's the funniest. *(laughs)*
Jojo	You're laughing.
Rocky	Yeah I saw the videos online – kentuckyfriedcruelty.com. It's a riot.
	(pause) Pamela Anderson's in the video too.
Jojo	Ah!
Rocky	*(laughs)* There's this one video where this guy is jumping on a chicken.
	It's so fucking funny man_
Jojo	You find that funny?
Rocky	Yeah! I mean... it's funny.
	(pause) It IS funny! It's just a chicken.
Jojo	Sure, that's ok then.
Rocky	It's a CHICKEN. It has an IQ of ten.
Jojo	You have an IQ of ten.
Rocky	You want to jump on me?
Jojo	That's not funny.

Rocky   I haven't been able to go to a disc.
         It's no fun anymore.

Jojo   Oh oh fucking calamity.
         You can't dance.
         You see cleavage and you think of me.
         You see ass and hips shaking and it's me again.
         Everything is black and white. Time feels like cough
         syrup…

Rocky   Remember the times we used to hang out after school?
         I value those times. I value_

Jojo   I'm not interested in the past.

Rocky   *(pause)* Get over it Jo.

(He punches hard.)

Rocky   Crap. One fifty.

Jojo   What's that supposed to mean?

Rocky   What's what?

Jojo   FUCK you you BASTARD you have no idea.

Rocky   I want us to move on. I need you to move on_

Jojo   It's so easy for you to say that. So incredibly easy.

Rocky   It's not.

Jojo   Not?

Rocky   I know you hate me.
         And that's why_ We're hanging out. Chilling.

Jojo   I hope YOU'RE having fun.

Rocky   I don't know what you want me to do?

Jojo   I want you to suffer.

Rocky   Oh man! Look at what that bastard has done to you? Where's Jojo? Who the fuck are you?

Jojo   It's not him. Don't kid yourself.

Rocky   Maybe this was a bad idea.
You need more time. I know what you're going through_

Jojo   Listen I'm going to tell dad. He doesn't know I've met you_

Rocky   There's no need to do that. I just wanted…

Jojo   I don't have to meet you.
I'm not interested. I'm doing you a favour.

Rocky   All you want is that freak show boyfriend of yours.
Oh look at me – I climb. I'm so cool I'm a monkey.
Let's run away and join the circus as trapeze artists.

Jojo   Fuck you and die.

Rocky   I'm going shopping. I'm sick of this.
I'm going to KFC and you can starve you stoned anorexic… FRUIT BAT.

(He punches hard. He throws away the glove.)

Rocky   Take the chits.
Buy yourself a fucking present.

(Rocky exits.)

IV

(Rocky paces trying not to punch anything.
He finds his pair of caterpillar boots, polishes them furiously.)

Rocky Fucking lunatic, lunatics – both of them.

(pause) My shoe rack used to be under the stairs. And under the stairs is where all the forgotten stuff in the house lands up. All the stuff you don't need anymore.

And once I was polishing my keds. And keds are an evil plot to keep you permanently occupied outside of school hours.

It's seven in the morning.

I'm smearing goopy white shoe polish all over my shoes.

And then I get up and POW.

One burst of red and then black. Complete black.

And I see that I've actually been putting BLACK WAX polish on the WHITE keds and I scream but the shoes start running away from me and I'm chasing them with the smell of phosphorous and black wax jammed under my fingernails.

Then I get up.

I've got this killer gash on my forehead.

I stood up and my head went straight into the back of the stairs.

I was out for twenty minutes.

So I run to school in wet keds and busted open forehead and stand in line.

And the prefects are checking everyone's shoes and I look down.

And my wound opens up again.

And plop plop. Two bright splotches of red on each white shoe.

This isn't a very good story is it?

Anyway… The point the point.

The moral of the story… and there must always be a moral.

Smash me on the forehead, and I'm out for twenty minutes.

(places his hand on his heart) Smash me here and it's all black. Black black…

V

(Zamiel and Priya enter panting from an ascent. They take in the view.)

Priya   It's perfect.

Zamiel   You're perfect.

Priya   You're exaggerating.
But… this makes the climb worth it. I love mountain air.
Wish I could take some back to the city with me.

Zamiel   I'm trying to forget about cities.

Priya   Forget it. And move on.

Zamiel   That's general advice.

Priya   Then give me details.

Zamiel   I'm planning to try and get a job.

(Priya laughs, controls herself.)

Priya   Sorry.

Zamiel   One of these corporate places has a sport climbing wall.
I could join there as an instructor. Money's good.

Priya   That's good.

Zamiel   No it's not.

Priya	Why not?
Zamiel	I don't want some fat executive's ass on my face as I'm holding him onto the bloody wall! And I'm not in the mood for the 'Oh you haven't got a degree' conversations either.
Priya	It will keep you occupied.
Zamiel	*(points)* See.
Priya	Oh my god, is that the lake where we went boating?
Zamiel	Yeah. *(pause)* This is keeping me occupied.
Priya	This is not work.
Zamiel	You're working.
Priya	That's different. I'm technically... well ok I am sort of working. Help me write my article.
Zamiel	What's it about?
Priya	Scenic Wayanad.
Zamiel	Wayanad is in Kerala. *(pause)* It is very scenic here.
Priya	Why did I ask! Let's see, I'll write about Chembara peak.
Zamiel	*(pause)* When are you getting back to REAL work?
Priya	I haven't decided. I like what I'm doing.
Zamiel	I'm sure you do.

Priya   *(pause)* I can't survive like this for long.
             All you do is whine about her this and her that and…
             I'm being patient.
             But I'm thinking about us now.
             This SMS thing doesn't work for me. I need the real
             you.

Zamiel   I don't think_

Priya   Yes. Exactly.
             Exactly the problem.

Zamiel   I can't seem to hold onto anything.
             I don't know what I'm supposed to do.

Priya   What do you want to do?

Zamiel   I don't know.

Priya   Then do what you do best.

Zamiel   I climb.

Priya   Then climb.

Zamiel   I am climbing.

Priya   Then shut up.
             And don't complain.

(Silence.)

Priya   You've woken up a fire in my belly that I thought shut
             down long ago.

Zamiel   You're old. You've got gas.

Priya   Shut up!
             I saw you climb at the South Zone Qualifiers and I
             knew you were trouble.

Zamiel   Oh that was fun.

Priya   Shut up. You were what… the first climber?

Zamiel   Yeah.

Priya   I was watching. That was a grade 9A route?

Zamiel   Nah – 4B.

Priya   Why did you do that?
So childish.

Zamiel   Because I could.

Priya   You ruined that competition for everyone you realise.

Zamiel   No man.

Priya   You did.
You made a mockery of the whole thing.
And you laughed at me when I met you first.

Zamiel   What! Some scruffy chick comes up to me and asks me if I have an attitude problem? What am I supposed to say?

Priya   Scruffy!

Zamiel   No no no no… dignified and learned… chick.

Priya   Thanks.

(Silence.)

Zamiel   I'm camping out here tonight.

Priya   I need to get back.

Zamiel   Stay.

Priya   After everything you've flung at me?

Zamiel   I'll make it up twice over.

Priya   All talk.

Zamiel   Are you tired?

Priya   The view's refreshed me. But…

Zamiel   I'll strap you onto my back.

Priya   *(laughs)* I won't fit in your backpack.

Zamiel   I'll rig you up properly.

Priya   Clown.

Zamiel   If you can survive another twenty minutes…

Priya   *(looks)* That's a sixty degree slope.

Zamiel   Stay with me. Just over that way is a tiny plateau.
It's off the main path.
There's a heart shaped aquifer there.
Gorgeous. A little heart shaped_ cool waters.
With the moon on it, the surface looks like crystal.
I've pitched my tent there. I'm staying the night.

Priya   The hotel will go mad.

Zamiel   First thing… daybreak I'll walk you right back down.
We'll tell the receptionist it got dark and you got lost.

Priya   Where did I spend the night?

Zamiel   You met a lover and talked all night.

Priya   I met a lover and TALKED?

Zamiel   You met an old friend and spent some time with him.

Priya	That's even worse_
Zamiel	You were seized with inspiration and wrote the whole night.
Priya	*(laughs)* You've made up your mind I see.
Zamiel	Come on. Done soaking up the view?
Priya	So are we off to talk or spend time or write?
Zamiel	My sleeping bag has some room. But we'll have to get rid of this stuff. Leave your shoes and socks on though.
Priya	*(laughs)* Oh my god! So that I won't freeze?
Zamiel	I assure you, that won't be a problem.
Priya	How about a midnight swim?
Zamiel	Er… it's an aquifer. The undertow… the currents, they'll pull you under. Take you underground to the base of the mountain.
Priya	Oh. That's not good.
Zamiel	And sometimes the wild animals come to drink there.
Priya	Right. I'm heading back to the hotel.
Zamiel	Oh come on. Race you to the top.

(He pulls her. They both head off laughing.
But Zamiel is too fast to keep up with.)

VI

(Priya is packing her belongings into boxes. She searches.
She finds a pair of red shoes.)

Priya   We wandered around a shopping mall.

We went up and down and up and down escalators.

Each city has its own character. Bombay is linear and in a hurry. Bangalore is all scattered and random. You feel each texture. Each city's aura.

But walk into a mall anywhere in India and it's all the same – even the air.

The stink of ac-perfumed soap on sale-fast food-generic deodorant stench.

Neon and plastic.

But with him, it made it tolerable.

I saw the shoes. And he's very quick on the uptake.

He said – 'You must never buy your lover shoes because they will walk away from you' and I laughed. 'So buy me chewing gum,' I said.

But he had made up his mind.

He bought me these red canvass shoes. And they're so infinitely comfortable.

But then it gets tricky… the choices I've made… the things I did…

(pause) I love these red shoes.

I'm very attached to them.

VII

(Zamiel plays with the carabiner. Puts on climbing shoes.
Rocky enters. He tries to cool down his arms.)

Rocky   Oh man... Totally pumped.

Zamiel   Overhang got you?

Rocky   Yeah. Crap crap crap.
             Just sapped me up completely.
             (looks, visualizes moves) I mean. Only a dyno can get
             you past that. Oof.

Zamiel   You been climbing long?

Rocky   Just started I guess.
             Saw the Qualifiers yesterday. Thought I'd try the route.
             I'll see if I can slip in the time next year to try.
             Get to the Nationals. But I've got a long way to go.

Zamiel   Go easy on the dynos.

Rocky   Yeah? Why?

Zamiel   You'll get hurt.

Rocky   I can take care of myself man.

Zamiel   Sure.

Rocky   You been climbing long?

Zamiel   About nine years.

Rocky   Oh shit. I'll take your advice then man.

Zamiel   Dynos damage your fingers in the long run.

Rocky   *(looks)* Just staying on, on that bloody overhang saps you.

Zamiel   Feels like heaven, but sucks you dry.

Rocky   *(pause)* You a sport climber?

Zamiel   Nope.

Rocky   Rocks?

Zamiel   Nope.

Rocky   Then?

Zamiel   I just climb. I love the mountains.

Rocky   Saw some guys take on this route yesterday.
It's a Grade 9A right? Bit tricky.
I spoke to the guy who won. He seemed really annoyed.

Zamiel   Yeah? Why?

Rocky   Some fucker took this route in 55 seconds.
Made everyone else look like crippled grannies in wheelchairs.

Zamiel   Oh yeah? He must have cheated.
It's a 60 foot wall.

Rocky   No man. He went first apparently.
He just treated the technical route like a power route.
Zoop he went, but the dumb fuck didn't clip in anywhere.

Didn't stop till the top, THEN clipped in and then came down upside down.

Zamiel   *(laughs)* What the fuck?

Rocky   Yeah. So he got disqualified.
Isn't that fucking surreal?

Zamiel   Yeah.

(Silence.)

Rocky   I know a friend of yours... Jojo.

Zamiel   *(pause)* Oh. Ah.

Rocky   Yeah, she goes on about you.
Says you climb like a lizard.
I thought I could learn some stuff from you.
She says you're pretty good.

Zamiel   You're the cousin.

Rocky   Yeah. I'm the cousin.
That's me.

Zamiel   Small world.

Rocky   Tiny.
Jojo and I go back since school.

Zamiel   You're down from Bombay.

Rocky   *(nods)* Dozens of tech jobs here in Bangalore.
Looking for placements.

Zamiel   I'm an outdoorsman.

Rocky   What do you do?

Zamiel   Climb.

Rocky   Just that?
Wow. Risky.

Zamiel   Much better than work work.

Rocky   There's conquest in business too.

Zamiel   Trading is about compromise.

Rocky   Ah. I can see what she sees in you.
(pause) You've gotten all edgy.

Zamiel   No.

Rocky   You're cool with me?

Zamiel   Yeah.

Rocky   Jo talks a lot.
I think I'll come back in the evening and try that route
again.
That overhang is pissing me off.

Zamiel   You're built for the rocks.

Rocky   Yeah?

Zamiel   The build.
Wall is mostly problem solving.
You'll feel free on the rocks.

Rocky   Cool cool. I can't wait to try it out.
How's Jo? I haven't met her in a while.

Zamiel   Same old Jo.
Bites your head off.

Rocky   Ha ha. Yeah, same old.

Zamiel   I'll tell her I met you.

Rocky   Yeah yeah sure. Whatever.
(pause) So I'm off then.

Zamiel   Good luck for the evening.

Rocky   Yeah. Will you be back?

Zamiel   I don't know.

Rocky   Ok. And tell me about any trips.

Zamiel   *(pause)* Might be heading out next month to Ramnagaram.

Rocky   Oh great great great. I'll join you.

Zamiel   Could try some easy routes for a start.

Rocky   Ok.
Damn… now this is going to be stuck in my head the whole day.

Zamiel   Plan a route.

Rocky   What?

Zamiel   On the technical route half the time you're going to have to traverse – move sideways. You've been watching the wrong pieces.
Those power holds, they're big and comfortable, they're rare on the rocks.
That is a pinch, it will tempt you on the overhang, but all it will do is sap you.

Rocky   Right right… Jo said you were a bit of a philosopher.

Zamiel   *(laughs)* The failed kind.

Rocky   What kind of name is Zamiel?

Zamiel   Zamiel – devil, angel of hurricanes?

Rocky   Cool shit man.

Zamiel   *(pause)* We might hang out some time.

Rocky   Great.

Zamiel   I'll bring Jo. We can chill.

Rocky   Not with Jo around.

Zamiel   *(laughs)* Yeah. Yeah that's true.
           Anyway got to go.

Rocky   Ok.

Zamiel   *(pause)* And…

Rocky   Sorry?

Zamiel   Try… right hand to green, left leg blue, reach with the
           left…

Rocky   Oooo!

Zamiel   Right leg up, swap, hip turn shift weight to lay back,
           left to pinch.
           Clip into the quickdraw.

Rocky   Holy fuck.

Zamiel   Yup.

(Rocky stays, trying to visualize the moves.
Zamiel walks off.)

VIII

(Zamiel plays with the carabiner. Climbs.)

Zamiel I started climbing when I was fifteen. I wanted to kill myself.

I started sport climbing.

And any idiot can tell you it's so safe, you're more likely to die crossing the road to get to the sports complex.

I loved it and then just went on to every other kind of climbing.

I'm the wrong build the wrong height the wrong temperament for every kind of climbing.

Guy called Muniraj taught me. '*Halliyantha hatthabeku!*' he would say.

Climb like the lizard!

He never understood how I was able to do it.

Neither did I back then…

Sometimes I would stay upside down on a roof or overhang.

Find a good hold, invert and relax.

And let all the blood go to my head.

And Muniraj would shout up and tell me to take down the carabiner on top when I was done and coil the rope.

And then he would just dump the belay and fuck off to get a coffee and a *beedi*!

Looking at the world upside down brings stunning clarity to everything.

Soon the urge to die vanished completely.
And I moved to the rocks. And then to the mountains.
Look I don't want to glorify the whole thing_
I just have a problem_ something's wrong with me....
And that's why I climb so well.
(pause) I have absolutely no idea how to let go.
(snaps the carabiner's gate open and closed)
Anyone who's moved in a relentlessly straight line will
tell you things move sideways.

IX

(Priya sits.
Jojo enters.)

Jojo   Priya?

Priya   Hi… hi.

Jojo   So it is you.

Priya   You're just like he described you.

Jojo   I thought you would be slightly younger.

Priya   (laughs) How old did you think I was?

Jojo   Not this old. (pause) I feel sick.

Priya   Have you gone to the doctor?

Jojo   Not that kind of sick.

Priya   Sit.

Jojo   What do you do?

Priya   I'm… on a break from work. (pause) I'm a counselor.

Jojo   That's kind of dumb. How much do you earn?

Priya   Enough.

Jojo   That's a shit pair of shoes.

Priya   They're comfortable.

Jojo	You travel a lot?
Priya	Of late.
Jojo	You sleep around a bit?
Priya	*(pause)* I'm very patient.
Jojo	Because your shoes, they look shit and they go all sorts of places. Are you the same?
Priya	*(pause)* Please sit. *(pause)* Is there something you want to tell me?

(Silence.)

Take your time.

Jojo	So he's on his own? Where is he?
Priya	I don't know. Anywhere. He's switched off. Is there something you would like to tell me?
Jojo	ARE YOU FUCKING TRYING TO COUNSEL ME?

(Silence.)

Don't take that tone_ don't try to counsel me.
I've had enough of counselors.

Priya	Would you PLEASE sit down?
Jojo	I just quit work today I'm going back to Bombay.
Priya	I'm so sorry to hear that. *(pause)* YOU called and asked to meet me here?
Jojo	God you sound like my mother. What the FUCK does he see in you?

(pause) He said you were a TISS grad.

Priya MSW. Medical and Psychiatric Social Work.
       I work with women and violence.

Jojo   *(laughs)* Good job. Great.
       Have YOU been abused?

Priya No_

Jojo   Then how the fuck do you know what it's like.
       You think you can fix me. Like something's wrong with
       me?

Priya *(laughs)* Oh my god…

Jojo   DON'T YOU FUCKING LAUGH AT ME.

(Jojo moves towards Priya, Priya tenses.
Jojo gives her a mobile phone. Priya reads the messages. Silence.)

Jojo   *(laughs)* This is priceless. He cheated on me with
       Mother Teresa.
       (pause) 'I love you. With you always forever.'

Priya Wayanad.
       He sent you this from Wayanad. I was with him.

Jojo   Yes. Came back all funny. Ramnagar?

Priya Yes. There was an accident, he fell… but_

Jojo   Yes he did. And you two met right here, at the
       Qualifiers.
       Which I didn't bother watching.
       (pause) Back of your neck goes cold. Blood turns to
       ice.
       It's your turn now.

Priya   I didn't know.
He told me you two broke up six months ago.

Jojo   We broke up six months ago.
When did he tell you this?

Priya   I can't remember exactly.

Jojo   Convenient. Just fucking great.
Senile Mother Teresa.

Priya   I didn't record every conversation I had with him.

Jojo   Maybe you should have.

Priya   So you two are still seeing each other?

Jojo   'Seeing each other' – what are you in college?

Priya   Are you in a committed relationship?

Jojo   Yes.

Priya   When?

Jojo   What when? Now.

Priya   How did you find out?

Jojo   You've slept with him.

(Silence.)

Jojo   What the fuck does he see in you? What the hell was he thinking?

(Priya is unable to read the rest. She returns the phone.)

Priya   This has come as a bit of a shock. I need some time to think.

Jojo   Why did you do this?

Priya	I didn't know.
Jojo	You're lying.
Priya	Yes I am.
Jojo	You admit it?
Priya	Will it make you happy if I was? *(pause)* You in your deranged need to pin it all down and label each part.
Jojo	You never knew a thing? Blissful ignorance.
Priya	I knew what he told me. Looking back nothing makes sense...

(Silence.)

	I love him.
Jojo	Even now.
Priya	Even now.
Jojo	I want you out of his life.
Priya	That's a harsh request.
Jojo	You've been lied to. WE've been lied to. Leave.
Priya	This is a nightmare.
Jojo	I'm five years of his life. We've gone to places together, you're never going to reach. You will never have what he and I share. He pieced me back together in a way no counseling will ever hope to do.

He and I looked death in the face.
You're a tourist. You're a visitor passing through.
You're a pothole on a very very long road.
Don't be pathetic – LEAVE.

Priya   I would like very much if you could_

Jojo   I'm done with you.

(Silence.)

Priya   Who did that to you?
(pause) He said you had an MTP. Was that a lie?

Jojo   What?

Priya   Medical termination of pregnancy.

(Silence.)

Jojo   So you know.

Priya   I don't know details.

Jojo   Do you want to compare notes?

Priya   I have to know. I just want to talk.
(pause) Please sit.

Jojo   So tangled. So unbelievably fucking tangled.

(She sits.)

X

(Zamiel enters, stops. Waits. Plays with the carabiner. Takes in the view.
Rocky enters panting, his Caterpillar boots slowing him down badly.)

Rocky How much further man? My feet are killing me.
Argh! Get these fucking things off me.

Zamiel We're halfway up.

Rocky Oh fuck me man.
You said that twenty minutes ago. I'm being massacred.

Zamiel We keep stopping, don't we?

Rocky Man I'm not a goat.
You think you're fucking Legolas or what?

(Rocky inspects himself for leeches, finds one near his ankle.)

Aargh! There's one on me there's one on me.
Get it off! Fuck off you bastard.

Zamiel Leave it.

Rocky That's my blood. I need it. I won't have this… TUBE
suck it all up for lunch.
Yuck yuck.
Oh wait, it's just a leaf.
(pause) Any more leech bites and I'm going to die of
blood loss.

Zamiel   We need to keep moving.

Rocky   Oh fuck off.

Zamiel   You're not really tired.

Rocky   No I'm not.
How the hell are you doing this? There's not a single one anywhere near you.

(Zamiel holds up his hands, he has his forefingers touching his thumbs.)

Zamiel   Do this.

Rocky   What the fucks that?

Zamiel   It affects your aura.
Leeches won't come near you.

Rocky   Man, you are like way loose...

Zamiel   We need to keep moving.

Rocky   We're taking a break.

Zamiel   We can't keep stopping.

Rocky   I say we can. I'm paying for this aren't I?
Now fuck you. You should have brought bug spray or salt or whatever.
(groans) My feet... Aargh here's another bastard! Gross gross gross.

Zamiel   We're in their territory.
(pause) Not the best things to wear on this kind of terrain.

Rocky   You know I'm sick of your fucking advice. Why don't you just shut it with your useful tips huh?

Tape your fingers for strength. Rubber sole shoes.
You're so fucking annoying man.

(Zamiel drinks water, offers Rocky some.)

Rocky   Fuck you man.

Zamiel   You'll dehydrate.

Rocky   Oh fuck you fuck you.

(Rocky snatches the water and drinks.)

Rocky   Wait wait let me guess.
If I drink too much I'm going to cramp up right. I'm
so sick of your shit.

(Silence. Zamiel lights up a beedi.)

Rocky   So tell me stuff.
If you're the guide you should be full of useful
information right?
You're supposed to be this great naturalist or
something.

Zamiel   What do you want to know?

Rocky   Entertain me asshole.

Zamiel   *(pause)* This is a mountain.

Rocky   Not good enough.
Why are all these leaves black? Are they diseased or is it
fungus or what?

Zamiel   They're decomposing. They fall from the trees, and rot.

Rocky   How enlightening.
See! That adds value to my trek.

Zamiel   If you say so.

Rocky   You know what your problem is you don't respect anything.
If you're providing a service you respect the customer. You serve.
(pause) So leeches also eat mud and shit it out right....
And they enrich the soil.

Zamiel   No. That's earthworms.

Rocky   Then what do leeches eat?

Zamiel   They're predators. They drink blood.

Rocky   So if I cut one in half will it like grow into two of them?

Zamiel   No. That's tapeworms.

Rocky   So what if I cut one open?

Zamiel   It will get cut open.
(pause) Then it might heal or die.

Rocky   And what about snakes? Are there rattle snakes?

Zamiel   We're in the Western Ghats!
This is a rain forest you idiot, we're not in the middle of a desert!

Rocky   Don't call me an idiot. You're the idiot.
Look at you sitting there. You're an embarrassment.
You call what you're doing a job? And you're doing even that so badly.
What are you achieving? Who the fuck cares whether you live or die?

(pause) How's Jo? Oh she left.

(pause) How's that other bitch... Priya? I saw you two at Ramnagar.

Oh, she left too.

I called Jo and had a chat with her. I told Jo what you were doing.

I told her that in college it's great to have this fashionable drop out freak show boyfriend. But the real world is different.

She deserves better than you.

She deserves someone who can take care of her, not someone who can barely survive on his own.

(pause) That means you're alone. No wait there's me, laughing at you, you sad pathetic failure of a person.

(Silence.

Rocky takes out his phone, searches for a signal.)

Rocky   Brilliant. There's signal.

(dials) Hi babes where you? I'm on a trek.

Some eight hours from Bangalore.

I can't pronounce the name of the place... peak is.... Hold on.

Oi! What's the name of the peak?

I'm asking you a question. What's the name of the peak?

Zamiel   Kumara Parvatha.

Rocky   Kumar Parvath... it's in the Malnad apparently.

Yeah it's good fun except for the leeches and the fuck all guide.

One of these outdoor types. Paid him some two thousand bucks and he's taking care of everything. He's a useless fucker otherwise....

He's out of work, took pity on him.

Yes babes it's safe. Really beautiful.

Anyway, take care. Just called to say hi. Ok. Ok bye.

(dials) Hey what's up! Nothing man. I'm up trekking in the mountains.

With some guy I hired... like one of these daily wage labourers.

Ha ha. Hey it's cool. I'll call you later. *(dials)*

(Zamiel puts out the beedi carefully, readies to continue the ascent, walks on.)

Rocky   Hey... where do you think you're going?

            (pause) I'm talking to you. I'm TALKING to you.

            Where do you think you're going?

(Rocky grabs Zamiel's backpack as he walks away.)

Rocky   Where do you think you're going?

Zamiel   Up.

Rocky   I'm not done here yet.

Zamiel   Ok.

Rocky   Which means you're not leaving yet...

Zamiel   No. I'm heading up.

Rocky   No you're not.

Zamiel   Yes I am.

Rocky   If you value your life, SHUT YOUR MOUTH and wait till I'm ready.

(*pause*) I brought you here… I BOUGHT you here to tell you something.

I want you to stay away from Jo.

Zamiel   What will you do?

Rocky   You want to know?

Zamiel   (*pause*)You've made your point.

(*Zamiel puts his backpack down.*)

Rocky   So we are clear then.

Zamiel   Crystal.

Rocky   Good that's good.

Zamiel   Good.

Rocky   So you'll stay away.

Zamiel   No.

Rocky   Are you playing with me?

Zamiel   What do you think?

Rocky   You said you'd STAY AWAY FROM HER!

Zamiel   I said you had made your point.

Rocky   You think I'm joking?

Zamiel   (*pause*) No.
(*pause*) I think you are a joke.

(*Rocky slams his hand across the side of Zamiel's face, catching him in the ear.*)

Rocky   Am I funny?

Zamiel   You don't want to go here.

Rocky   Why? You scared?

(Rocky laughs. Gets a call.
Zamiel sticks his finger in his ear, trying to get some hearing back.
No luck.)

Rocky   Hey. No man I'm not in town. I'm out trekking.
             Yeah, I can talk for a bit. No not busy at all. Tell me.

(He takes Rocky's phone and tosses it far away.)

Rocky   What the FUCK MAN! THAT'S MY PHONE.

Zamiel   She told me what you did to her.

Rocky   My phone! She's lying_

Zamiel   Why did you do it? You think you have strength?

Rocky   Look at you. Fucking loser accusing me of all this. And
             do you know how much that phone cost me?

Zamiel   I'll buy you another.
              Did you like it? Fucking her crying and screaming.

Rocky   One more word and you're dead. My phone!

Zamiel   You are in no FUCKING position to want anything or
              ask anything of me.

Rocky   She got pregnant… flipped out on me. It was an
             accident.

Zamiel   Ok man… let's stop ok. You're sounding pathetic
              now.

Rocky   I didn't do anything WRONG!

(Rocky punches wildly. Zamiel barely manages to deflect it, dropping the carabiner in the process. Rocky attacks Zamiel, they grapple. Zamiel manages to lock up Rocky in a rear naked chokehold. Rocky fumes, spits and struggles but cannot break the hold.)

Zamiel   Calm down. I don't want to do this. This won't solve anything.

(Rocky struggles, gives up. Zamiel releases the lock and gets to his feet.
Rocky begins to cry. Zamiel gives him water.)

Rocky   Every day man every day. We were like best friends.
Not one day when we didn't talk to each other.
And then she starts talking about you. And I could feel her slipping away. I was on fucking medication, after she stopped talking to me.
And then you were giving her a hard time and then one day she came crying to me. And we were home. And it went all wrong. And then she got pregnant.
And I didn't know what to do. It's all fucked.
I can't be without her. What the fuck am I supposed to do about that?
And I've seen her twice in six months. And she's someone else.
And I met her once. Once before this.
And I tried to make it like it was. But I couldn't.

Zamiel   *(pause)* She said she came over confused to talk.
You got all weird.
She said no.
You didn't stop.

Rocky   So fucking convenient.
Make me the monster.

Zamiel   If she didn't get pregnant would she have told the same story?

Rocky   I don't know!
She was never like this.
Not before you.

Zamiel   She is me.
We're the same.
Carbon fucking copy.

(Zamiel gently picks a leech off his foot.)

Zamiel   We have the same fucking tenacity.
(pause) These things are ruthless. A mouth, a stomach and teeth.
You don't feel anything when it's on you.
But pull it off and your flesh comes with it.
And the wound won't close.
Together – and you're slowly draining. Apart and… you drain away…

(Silence.)

Zamiel   All I can do is climb.
That's who I am. That's all I have left.
When I climb I'm a God.

(Zamiel walks to his backpack. Rocky blinks in disbelief at the last statement.
Rocky picks up the fallen carabiner, slips it onto his fist.
Punches Zamiel on the back of the head, taking him down.)

Rocky   YOU ARE NOTHING!
YOU ARE NO ONE!
NO ONE.
I'M A FUCKING HUMAN BEING.
I'M FUCKING HUMAN.

(He crushes Zamiel's hand under his boots, breaking all the fingers.)
FUCK YOU AND DIE.

Act 2

(Zamiel tries to get to his feet. Can't.
He sees the fallen carabiner, tries to pick it up. Drops it.
He tries again. Drops it.
He concentrates, picks it up, tries to snap the gate, drops it.
Blackout.
Zamiel huddled to keep warm.
He writes a letter, with a hand that won't cooperate.)

Zamiel   Delhi – Rishikesh – Uttarakashi – Gangotri. Bhagiriti – raging blue, so pure. Chirbasa Bhojbasa Gaumukh Tapovan Nandanvan Shivling.

Moving like lightning – up too fast. Too fast. Haven't acclimatized. I'm burnt.

I can't hold onto anything. I'm bleeding memories.

Kheda Taal.

Somewhere in that mess of a journey back down, the Baba asked me – 'Why?'

And I remember mumbling –

'I climb, because I want to come down again.'

Listen to me.

You know me. I just don't know when to quit.

(pause)

But there's more stars here than I've ever seen in my life.

And the sky bends, it's like running my hand along your back, Jo.

I fucked up. I'm sorry.

(Jojo puts a boxing glove on Zamiel's bleeding hand.)

Jojo   My tough man. My Hindi film hero.

Zamiel   Laugh laugh.

Jojo   You can just buy me something.

Zamiel   I have to win it for you. The effort counts.

Jojo   But you needn't_

Zamiel   Too late damage done.

(Zamiel takes a deep breath. Punches the bull's-eye hard. He jumps up and down screaming expletives, clutching the glove.)

Jojo   Baby lover baby sweetheart.

Zamiel   What was it?

Jojo   Are you ok?

Zamiel   The score the score you cow…

Jojo   A hundred and thirty kgs.

Zamiel   Aaaargh! The bastard was on steroids.

Jojo   He was wearing tight jeans too. He was a loser.

Zamiel   The chick he was with was hot.

Jojo   She's got blonde written all over her.

Zamiel   Ok ok. Two more.

Jojo   Yeah. That's it and we've won.

Zamiel   I'll just keep it at the same score.

Jojo   I've got a job in Bangalore.

Zamiel   You're trying to distract me.

Jojo   No. I'm serious.

Zamiel   That's brilliant! What?

Jojo   Some IT rubbish I don't know.
It will keep me close to you. That's all I care.

Zamiel   That's cool.
Now I HAVE to win something for you.

(Silence. Zamiel focuses.)

Jojo   That's cool?
Is that all you have to say?

Zamiel   Yeah. It is cool.
Why? What am I supposed to say?

Jojo   I'm moving to another city to be close to you.

Zamiel   If that's what you want to do.

Jojo   *(pause)* Never mind.

Zamiel   What? What the hell does distance have to do with anything.
If you feel you'll be closer to me if you're in Bangalore, fine.

Jojo   I don't understand you. Never mind.
Let's talk about something else.

Zamiel   Hitting one-fifty.

Jojo   The one fifty doesn't matter.

Zamiel   Now why did you go and say that?

Jojo	What?
Zamiel	That one fifty doesn't matter? He hit one fifty.
Jojo	So what?
Zamiel	I can hit one fifty.
Jojo	Sure you can.
Zamiel	Yeah. *(pause)* And your hair is much sexier than that blonde's…
Jojo	*(pause)* What's wrong with my hair?
Zamiel	It's gorgeous.
Jojo	What's different about it?
Zamiel	*(pause)* No no no that's not fair that's not fair…
Jojo	I don't know why I bother.
Zamiel	That's cheating baby. How am I supposed to answer that?
Jojo	This is the last time I bother dressing up for you.
Zamiel	*(pause)* Your eye shadow is different? *(pause)* Your anklet_ No wait. One of your moles has moved?
Jojo	Last time.
Zamiel	Give me clue.
Jojo	It's the hair clip YOU bought me_
Zamiel	I knew that I knew that. But I saw you this morning as well_

Jojo	Forget it_
Zamiel	I mean how was I supposed to… I mean I'm not staring at the back of your head as of now.
Jojo	Drop it. *(pause)* I'm waiting for my prize.
Zamiel	Yes ma'am. I set my mind on something I'll get it done. And this will be the first of many gifts. We need to go on that world tour too. It will be a blast.

(Silence.
Zamiel takes a run up. Punches harder than the first time. Staggers back.)

Jojo	Oooooooo! One forty five.
Zamiel	FUCK!
Jojo	You did it now let's go.
Zamiel	I've figured it out. It's in the wrist.
Jojo	Good now come let's select my prize.
Zamiel	How many chits?
Jojo	Two seventy five! We can get something really nice. I got my eye on a cute teddy.
Zamiel	One more punch. I've got one more punch to hit one fifty.
Jojo	My prize.
Zamiel	The prize yes, and the effort.
Jojo	*(pause)* Ok forget the prize.
Zamiel	No no no. One fifty one fifty.

Jojo	I'll still love you just as much if you don't hit one fifty.
Zamiel	And I'll love you twice as much after.
Jojo	So you only love me halfway now?
Zamiel	Yeah. *(pause)* Because you're obsessed with gifts. And you talk too much.
Jojo	*(pause)* I'm leaving, Bye see you!
Zamiel	No no no no no. It's not bad.
Jojo	What the hell do you mean?
Zamiel	What? You are.
Jojo	Am not.
Zamiel	You'd like a little house wouldn't you? With a small lawn for cosy little parties with friends. And a dishwasher. And hardwood flooring. And a nice well stocked bar with lots of yummy liqueurs. And_
Jojo	Who wouldn't want all that?
Zamiel	I don't want all that.
Jojo	Of course you do. You just went all poetic about it.
Zamiel	No. I just... pointed out the futility of that want.
Jojo	What's futile about it?
Zamiel	What will you do with it?
Jojo	Live in it!
Zamiel	With who?
Jojo	With you of course.

Zamiel   No.

Jojo   What no?

Zamiel   I'm going to be in my shack in the mountains.

Jojo   During summer. The rest of the time you can be with me.

Zamiel   So you want to spend only half your time with me?

Jojo   Ah! Got me.

Zamiel   Anyway… I love getting you gifts. And we're fucking off on our world tour the moment we can.

Jojo   I love your gifts.

Zamiel   See. You love the gifts.

Jojo   I love them because you gave them to me.

Zamiel   That's on second thought…

Jojo   Are you going to talk or get me my gift?

Zamiel   I was taking a break. *(touches her cheek)* See, how she leans her cheek upon my hand! O, that I had not this glove so that I may touch that cheek!

Jojo   Talk talk talk!

Zamiel   I'm being poetic.

Jojo   You're avoiding the task at hand.

Zamiel   Babes?

Jojo   Yeah?

Zamiel   You're my last girlfriend. You're the one. I'm with you forever. Till I die. Forever and ever. And so on and so forth.

Jojo   I believe you.

Zamiel   I'll do anything for you.

Jojo   I know baby.

(Silence.
Zamiel takes a deep breath. Takes a run up. Punches even harder.)

Jojo   One fifty one! My god you're insane. *(laughs)* Come come. Let's get my prize. We've got… four hundred and twenty six chits! We might be able to pay cash and get something in the four fifty range… Come come come. We'll be late.

(She removes the glove.
Rocky takes the glove from her.
He stares at his reflection in his pair of caterpillar boots, polishes them.)

Rocky   I stole this. One of those dumb things you do when you're not thinking clearly. I do that a lot. It's to commemorate the day I hit one fifty for her. Later I found out that Z hit one fifty too. Don't know how he managed that. *(pause)* I thought I killed him that day. I ran down the mountain. Left him there in the mud. I never found my fucking phone. It started raining. Ran down with the mud and slush streaming downhill. Leeches had a field day.

Five or six of them. Fat with my blood. I reached the base and scraped them all off me with a stone. They fell off, wriggled away.

I cut them open with the stone. They crawled away from me leaving bright red trails of my blood.

This is my life I said. These are my choices.

This is me sitting here angry enough to kill him.

This is me who never hurt Jo, who was strong enough to stop myself, who stayed her friend and caught up with her ten years later to laugh at the rubbish we did.

This is me who let it all go and became a stronger person and realized this makes no difference in the larger scheme of things.

And this is me who shut my mouth and didn't run like a schoolgirl to tell Jo stuff that made no sense and well and truly fucked it all up for everyone. Who just turned away because he was a better man.

This is me who can live with myself.

He came down later. We got on the bus. Eight hours of absolute silence. Malnad to Bangalore. Every time the bus hit a bump he winced, holding one hand with the other. We landed in the city and he just took out an envelope and gave me back my money. I couldn't even look at him. I can't even look at myself.

(He throws away the glove.
Priya ties her shoelaces.
Rocky enters.)

Rocky   Hi Priya.

Priya   Oops! Hi.

Rocky   Name's Rocky.

Priya   Rocky? Rocky…

Rocky   Cause I climb rocks.

Priya   *(laughs)* That's very funny. *(pause)* You're serious.

Rocky   Rahul. But call me Rocky.

Priya   *(pause)* You're Jojo's cousin.

Rocky   You're saying it like now you don't want to have anything to do with me.

Priya   *(pause)* Not at all. Just surprised.

Rocky   Why?

Priya   Memories…

Rocky   *(laughs)* Yes yes. I know.

Priya   You climb?

Rocky   No. I gave up. Don't have the time anymore. Busy busy busy. Just dropped in to see the Qualifiers. Nothing interesting.

Priya   No. Just the usual.

Rocky   Just thought I'd watch a few climbers. You?

(He furiously polishes his shoes.)

Priya   Sorry?

Rocky   What brings you here?

Priya   I… same reason I guess.

Rocky   Exciting route?

Priya   The route was alright, but the climbs were a bit boring. No fireworks. *(pause)* I've met you before. Once… in Ramnagaram right?

Rocky   That's right. *(pause)* Saw you with Z a while ago.

Priya   Ok.

Rocky	Yes… Zamiel. If you'd rather not talk about any of this.
Priya	It's fine.
Rocky	I've been working on my temper you know.
Priya	Ok.
Rocky	You know, so I can talk about stuff without getting upset you know.
Priya	Ok.
Rocky	I'm a very angry person… so I'm trying to be moderate.
Priya	Ok.
Rocky	Yes. I'm very calm now. I can't stand dirt on these things. I like to see my reflection in them.

(He furiously polishes his shoes.)

Priya	That's great Rahul_ Rocky.
Rocky	The Ramnagar trip was good. Barring that little mishap.
Priya	Ah yes. That was a good trip.
Rocky	You're a good medic. That was some quick thinking and patch work.
Priya	I studied a little first aid. It came in handy.
Rocky	Yeah. That's my memory of you. Not even batting an eyelid with all that skin burnt off. And just getting it all cleaned. And Zamiel just staring at you with one look in his eyes_

Priya   Yes. I remember that.

Rocky   Are you seeing someone now?

Priya   *(laughs)* My god you're still serious…

Rocky   I am.

Priya   *(points)* Guy in the blue shirt with glasses. Raj.

Rocky   Ah ok. He's ok.

Priya   Thank you.

Rocky   I mean. He's normal. He looks normal.

Priya   Rocky?

Rocky   You know… straight. Not gay straight. Sort of… straightforward.
(pause) I've been troubled of late you know.

Priya   Yes Rocky… what has been troubling you?

Rocky   Thank you thank you. I know Jo really well. Do you know her?

Priya   Met her briefly, but intensely.

Rocky   Yes yes. Exactly my point.

(He furiously polishes his shoes.)

Priya   Sorry?

Rocky   I'm normal right?

Priya   What's not normal about you?

Rocky   Because those two you know… they're insane. Totally fucking off.

Priya   They were. Yes. I wouldn't really know. I was caught in a mess...

Rocky   No no. Yes. I know. But they were not all there you know...

Priya   Yes. I suppose. Are you ok?

Rocky   Something_ Two things have been bothering me a lot. I thought I would tell you those things.

Priya   My god you're in a hurry.

Rocky   Really? I'm not being moderate?

Priya   No no you are...

Rocky   I don't mean to offend you.

Priya   No offence just... ok. You want to have this talk, we will. Just take it easy.

Rocky   I'm a wreck you know. I'm glad I saw you. It's been eating into me.

Priya   I haven't dealt with this in a while.

Rocky   I'm sorry. I'm very sorry.

Priya   For what?

Rocky   I saw you two together and I told Jo about you two. And... I wasn't thinking clearly at the time. And... that's how this whole thing came to this mess. If I had just shut my mouth, and let go, none of this might have happened.

(Silence.
Rocky regards his reflection.)

Priya	It doesn't matter Rocky. It's in the past. I'm moving_ I have moved on.
Rocky	Because it went really ugly_
Priya	I know. But what happened happened. I'm glad it did.
Rocky	It's been eating me. Thought I'd come back here one more time to close it all.
Priya	I guess I'm doing the same.
Rocky	Because I was really angry at the time...
Priya	It's fine. I'm glad I knew the truth in the end.
Rocky	Oh... Truth?
Priya	If I had never known, it would have... been difficult later.
Rocky	In what sense?
Priya	I'm glad I found out when I did before I made any big decisions.
Rocky	About?
Priya	About my life.
Rocky	Ok. You don't think I'm evil do you?
Priya	No.
Rocky	I'm normal right?
Priya	Are any of us?
Rocky	What's that supposed to mean?
Priya	Nothing.

Rocky   You hate my guts too DON'T YOU?

Priya   I don't know you.

Rocky   Wait wait.. I'm sorry, I'm so sorry. *(pause)* I just get a little carried away. I'm not like her. I'm different. I'm moderate.

(He furiously polishes his shoes.)

Rocky   Squeaky clean.

Priya   No problem.

Rocky   And I'm sorry but whatever she told you about me is a lie.

Priya   *(pause)* I don't know what you mean.

Rocky   Did she talk to you about me?

Priya   *(pause)* Not really.

Rocky   Are you sure?

Priya   Now you are sounding like her.

Rocky   No then. Great ok. That's it.

Priya   Great.

Rocky   I'm normal. I've been working hard. Far away. Just focussing on career.

Priya   That's good.

Rocky   What does Raj do?

Priya   He's not a climber if that's what you meant. *(pause)* He's HR.

Rocky	Oh excellent excellent. *(pause)* How is Z's hand?
Priya	Sorry what? I don't know.
Rocky	Nothing nothing just worried about him.
Priya	Ok. How is Jo?
Rocky	Lost touch. Well anyway, nice meeting you. I'm off. All the best. Dust settles.
Priya	Ok. See you.

(He exits furiously polishing his shoes.
Priya looks at her shoes.)

Priya	Why do I give people the benefit of the doubt?
	Because there is no objective truth. There is no what really happened.
	I make choices. Some of them I am proud of. Some of them I am not.
	It wasn't easy walking away from everything. What else could I do? Just break every connection and move away. I can't separate the lies from the truth, so I take all that I have and I put it away and try to move on. *(pause)* How easy to laugh at Rocky's attempts to cover up his past.
	How easy to write off Jojo with a hundred convenient labels?
	And Z… I never tested him. No cross questions, side steps, double guesses.
	I trusted him. And…
	I can't bring myself to judge people. Because we never have the whole picture. You know nothing other than what I tell you and you assume the rest.

(pause) Will you judge me if I tell you that Raj who I delicately claim is my boyfriend is my husband? I'm moving back in with him.

Don't judge me.

(pause) I'm getting back to work. For some reason I feel slightly stronger, a little less tired. It's not easy listening to the stories out there, but I do what I can. I do my little bit.

But things keep coming back...

Zamiel...

Green boots – what are you thinking?

(Jojo returns a box to Zamiel.
Zamiel can barely hold it. He drops it and a pair of slippers falls out.
He puts them back in the box with great effort.)

Zamiel	Ow. Ow. No no. I insist you take these.
Jojo	I don't want it.
Zamiel	Will you focus?
Jojo	Ok. Focussed.
Zamiel	We've got Afghan church booked. I got rid of the Crystal Ball Room at The Taj idea. I got the Salt Water Grill on Marine Drive. I've pulled a favour with a friend. We can do a theme if you like. Check out the invitations... Now...
Jojo	Did you invite Priya?
Zamiel	I called her. She didn't take my call.
Jojo	And your parents?

Zamiel   No.

Jojo   What kind of invitations are these?

Zamiel   The border has come out gorgeous.

Jojo   You've not invited half the list.

Zamiel   I have.

Jojo   It's so gaudy.

Zamiel   Rubbish. Everyone on the list has been invited.

Jojo   I'm sure you've forgotten half the important people.

Zamiel   No I haven't.

Jojo   You've missed something.

Zamiel   No. I got it all covered.

Jojo   I don't want this gift.

Zamiel   I don't want it either.

Jojo   Then what?

Zamiel   Then leave it here. The flower guy will confirm tomorrow.

Jojo   Ok.

Zamiel   Have you booked your parlour timings?

Jojo   That you leave to me dear.

(Silence.)

Zamiel   *(smiles)* I went shopping for something to wear at the reception. Bummed about on Linking Road.

Jojo   Did you get something nice?

Zamiel   No. I tried on about four suits and then ran out screaming.

Jojo   Typical. I've not been keeping well. I'm not well at all actually.

Zamiel   I bought you this pair of chappals. Nice bling joothis.

Jojo   Ah. You know my taste.

Zamiel   I bought myself a pair of shoes too. Now I'm broke.

Jojo   What?

Zamiel   Kaos.

Jojo   Oh no.

Zamiel   So no suit. But check out what it says on the manual – Excellent for smearing, toe holds and wet grips. NOT FOR BEGINNERS. You know things are in a different league when you have shoes that have manuals.

Jojo   Then what are you going to wear at the reception?

Zamiel   A pair of jeans and a tee-shirt.

Jojo   I'll have security remove you. Or beat you up at the gate. *(pause)* How are the kids?

Zamiel   Good. They keep calling me uncle. Some of them are incredible climbers. I'll miss them. *(pause)* You don't wear those till after the wedding ok.

Jojo   Ok. Why won't Priya come? I'd really like her to be there.

Zamiel   I don't want to force anything. Let it go.

Jojo   I got stoned yesterday.

Zamiel   I can see. *(pause)* Well… I hope it was a good trip?

Jojo   I'm still a little elsewhere.

Zamiel   Yeah. I'll just see you through this and I'll be a little elsewhere as well. I didn't know you were back on the weed. Was that your last chance for a free ride?

Jojo   No. He's cool.

Zamiel   I like him a lot.

Jojo   My parents are in love with him.

(Silence.)

Jojo   Where will you be after…

Zamiel   I'm heading back… onto some new routes.

Jojo   You just came back from the north.

Zamiel   I came back for you.

Jojo   Aren't you going to try and stop me?

(Silence.)

Zamiel   No. You're free to do what you want.

(Silence.)

Zamiel   I'll leave.

(Zamiel leaves.)

Jojo   *(pause)* When an ant dies it releases a scent. Other ants come and pick him up and put him with all the other dead ants. If you rub the scent on a live ant, he's dead to everyone else. He'll try to go about his normal routine.

But he's dead. He moves and breathes... but for all
practical purposes to the rest of the colony he's dead.

(Priya reads a letter.
Silence.
She dials a number. A phone rings.
Rocky answers.)

Priya   This can't be happening.

Rocky   I'm sorry.

Priya   He was alone? No belayer?

Rocky   Yeah. I'm sorry to have... been the one to tell you.

Priya   But it's Z... he can't...

Rocky   It was an accident. The equipment failed.

Priya   What?

Rocky   It failed on an overhang somewhere in Lonavala.

Priya   But...

Rocky   I mean... what was he thinking... he was climbing
alone? And his hand was... *(pause)* Look... I'm sorry.
Everyone's shocked. It's over... he's... I don't know
man. That letter was for you. It was in his back pack. I
need to give some other stuff to Jo some time.

Priya   Does she...

Rocky   Yeah.

Priya   Is she ok?

Rocky   No. She's not. Jo is Jo. She stopped eating. She's in the
hospital. On drips. She's terrible. I'll give her the stuff

later. I mean... it will just kill her. *(pause)* Oh fuck I can't believe I said that.

Priya Did you go see her?

Rocky Kind of. I mean, I went there. Met... Amjad. Her husband. What an asshole. *(pause)* I love the guy. He's been there for her right through. Never left her side. She treats him like shit. I just felt unnecessary. I'll wait till she's stronger.

Priya I'm glad you gave me these.

Rocky Man I'm so sorry. I've met you twice and both times it's been utterly fucked.

Priya I'm glad you think I'm strong enough.

Rocky It's like carrying a bomb. You can keep it. Why can't things be fluffy all the time? Yeah? Where the fuck did all the happy people go? Where did they vanish? Who fucking stole my cotton candy? *(pause)* Sorry. *(pause)* Been on anymore trips?

Priya No. Raj can't handle it. And I don't feel like going alone.

Rocky Yeah. I'm fucking off next month. Cardiff. Going off to do a one year masters. Business. It'll keep my mind off things.

(Silence.)

Priya Rocky... something's not right...

Rocky He's gone. She's shit. We're permanently head fucked. Yeah. *(pause)* Lots of stuff isn't right.

Priya   What?

Rocky   I'm going to go to hell for this...

Priya   What?

Rocky   The bastard just wouldn't quit...

Priya   Please... I know. But please don't talk about him like that.

Rocky   I'm sorry but after Jo...

Priya   I'm sure it's been difficult for you.

Rocky   No. After Jo... He... I think he just ran out of steam.

Priya   He was planning on travelling.

Rocky   I think we know him. We both know him. He went on a huge trip up north apparently. He fell sick. Came back... then just went straight back onto the rocks. Really crazy routes. Refused to climb with anyone else. *(pause)* He couldn't QUIT. Promise me you'll not tell anyone else this. I'm only telling you this because you deserve to know... Other climbers were telling me stuff. He went climbing alone. Not in any shape to climb. He used an old crab. It had a hairline crack in it. He knew it was fucked up... He knew it wouldn't take another fall.

(Silence.
Rocky gets another call.)

Rocky   I'll try to keep in touch. Ok. You take care. You stay rock solid. Bye. Yup. Hi man what's up. No man, I'm free to talk. Well it did jump 427 points this morning.

Yes. Well it depends… Which fund manager are you talking to…

(Rocky leaves.
Priya smiles.
A very long silence.
She begins to weep uncontrollably.
She takes off her red shoes and packs them into the box, tapes the box closed.
She leaves.
Zamiel stares at the sun for an eternity.)

Zamiel   Staring right into the sun.
Everything breaks…

(runs his finger right around the carabiner)

Anyone who's moved in a relentlessly straight line will tell you things move in circles.

(Jojo is looking for something.
She's stoned, crying, freezing.)

Jojo   We went to the Eiffel tower yesterday. It's a sniffle. Went to the Eiffel tower. He has a meeting so I'm just sitting in the hotel. It's a Novotell.
I spat over the edge. Just the first floor, no time to go higher. Then I threw a 25-franc coin over the edge…. People looked like ants.
I have an a.c. in my room. And a radiator. And a mini fridge. And a view of the Seine. And hardwood flooring. And lots of liqueurs.
I spat over the edge. A 25-franc coin spinning…

(Zamiel hugs her from behind.

Moments before sunset.
Zamiel and Jojo lean on the ledge.)

Jojo   Any minute now.

Zamiel   The best one I've seen in a while.

Jojo   Mmm. I can imagine the best.

Zamiel   Red ball of a sun. Plunging into the sea. And I was walking along the beach. Every twenty seconds I'd glance right and it would have moved. But you don't see the movement. Sun in the sky like a crab in the water.

Jojo   That's amazing. God. There are so many things I want to share with you.

Zamiel   No hurry.

Jojo   No hurry? No hurry! Of course there is.

Zamiel   Well that's one approach.

Jojo   There's never enough time. And always the wrong space.

Zamiel   You have to go back to work?

Jojo   Screw work.

Zamiel   *(pause)* I've got you a gift.

Jojo   Yay! Another one? I feel guilty. What is it?

Zamiel   Secret.

Jojo   No no.

Zamiel   Surprise.

Jojo   Clue.

Zamiel   It's not physical.

Jojo   An imaginary gift?

Zamiel   Um… it's metaphysical.

Jojo   Oh help. *(pause)* A kiss?

Zamiel   That's close… but a kiss… even my kisses are still physical. I'm working on the metaphysical kisses though.

Jojo   So I don't get one?

Zamiel   *(kisses her)* Whenever you need one. I always have stock.

Jojo   Mmm. SO what is the gift?

Zamiel   Still haven't figured it out?

Jojo   It's not something nasty is it?

Zamiel   Depends.

Jojo   Oh no. I'm in trouble.

Zamiel   You're with me aren't you?

Jojo   Oh why why why?

Zamiel   *(laughs)* Haven't a clue. Paying for your past sins.

Jojo   Must have been terrible crimes!

Zamiel   Absolutely.

Jojo   Darling.

Zamiel   Baby Jo. *(holds her)* Squishy.

Jojo	Fat baby Jo.
Zamiel	Who cares there's more of you to hold.
Jojo	So I'm fat?
Zamiel	What? You mean in the head? Or_
Jojo	Oh shut up.
Zamiel	Ok ok.

(Silence.)

Jojo	Are you going to get around to it?
Zamiel	I'm contemplating.
Jojo	Ok I'll just go then and leave you to contemplate.
Zamiel	I'm wondering whether I'm… we are ready for it?
Jojo	O… K. Can you tell me what it is?
Zamiel	It's not a verbal thing.
Jojo	Oh god get on with it!
Zamiel	Fine. Ready or not… If this gift is going to work, you'll have to co-operate. And trust me… absolutely.
Jojo	What are you going to do?
Zamiel	Non-verbal.
Jojo	You've got my curiosity. Just don't hurt me.

(Zamiel sweeps her off her feet into his arms.
Jojo shrieks.)

Jojo	Put me down put me down.

Zamiel Close your eyes for gods sake and no kicking you'll ruin it.

Jojo I'm heavy, you'll hurt your back.

Zamiel You're a baby.

Jojo It's not something kinky is it?

Zamiel Stop blabbering.

Jojo I want to be put down.

Zamiel Then no gift.

Jojo Fucking hell, why make it so difficult?

Zamiel Just relax, see I got you.

(Zamiel spins her around.
Rocks her gently. Her kicking subsides.)

Zamiel I've got you my goddess.

Jojo You're insane.

Zamiel Totally. Mad about you.

Jojo I'm wondering whether I want this gift.

Zamiel Too late. See nothing to fear. I want you to shut up for a bit.

Jojo But what_

Zamiel Shut up!

Jojo Fine I'm going to sleep.

Zamiel Good girl.

(He walks in circles, rocking her.

Jojo enjoys the ride quietly.
Deftly Zamiel steps up and onto the ledge, puts Jojo down, takes a
step back.)

Zamiel   I love you. Open your eyes. Come here. *(pause)* Come.
(pause) Take my hand. Trust me.

(Long silence.
She takes a step.
Zamiel kisses her.
Silence.
She begins to cry. Zamiel helps her down.
She refuses to stand. They both sink to their knees.)

Zamiel   My darling my baby…

(Jojo sniffles. Then attacks Zamiel.
Zamiel hugs her and smothers her swats.)

Jojo   You have no right to do that. No right.

Zamiel   I love you.

Jojo   You could have KILLED US BOTH!

Zamiel   I love you.

Jojo   Fuck you. Fuck you you lunatic.

Zamiel   I love you.

Jojo   Stop saying that, it's not an excuse.

Zamiel   I love you.

(Silence.)

No matter what happens. Remember that feeling in
your stomach. Just remember that… instant of absolute

stillness. Of terror and excitement, of shock and rapture, and my unbearable ravenous all consuming love for you. That's my gift.

(Silence.
She swats him.)

Jojo   Why couldn't you just buy me flowers?

Zamiel   They look pretty, but then... after a few days. This instant is with you forever.

Jojo   You're going to kill me.

Zamiel   Never.

Jojo   For sure.

Zamiel   No. You'll never feel this alive ever again.

(Silence.)

Zamiel   We missed it.

Jojo   Gone?

Zamiel   Gone.

Jojo   Sorry we didn't see it.

Zamiel   There'll be another tomorrow.

Jojo   Pretty?

Zamiel   Yes. Very pretty...

END

HARD PLACES

Farhad Sorabjee

About the Playwright

Farhad Sorabjee is a Mumbai-based writer. *Hard Places* was premiered in Mumbai as part of the 'Writers' Bloc' festival for new Indian writing in 2004, was part of the Eurotopiques theatre festival in Lille in May, 2010, and is slated for production in the U.K. in 2012. Productions of his work have been staged at theatres in India and his work has been read at the Royal Court Theatre and the Soho Theatre in London. His work was produced as part of '36 Ghante', a multi-lingual festival of plays by prominent writers, directors and actors in India. He has also written a novel, which is scheduled for publication in 2012.

Hard Places

Hard Places was first presented at the Prithvi Theatre, Mumbai on April 18ᵗʰ 2004, produced by Rage Productions. The cast was as follows:

Aziz   Nadir Khan

Saira   Faezeh Jalali

Mother   Dipika Roy

Director   Rooky Dadachanji

Set Designer   Arzan Khambatta

Lighting Designer   Inaayat Ali Sami

Acknowledgements

Thanks to everyone involved with the development and life of this play; in particular to Carl Miller, Phyllida Lloyd, the three magnificent musketeers of Rage Productions, Rookie Dadachanji and his wonderful cast, Rebecca Gould, Chris White. And most of all, for the unstinting encouragement of my wife, Anu.

Playwright's Note

The genesis of *Hard Places* lies in a short television report that I saw on a news programme about a place in the Golan Heights called the Shouting Valley.

Cutting across the Shouting Valley is a border fence erected by Israel, which divides Syrian-held territory from Israeli-held territory annexed by it during the Six Day War in 1967. The border fence cut families and homesteads apart, dividing and separating them from each other forever. These families routinely stand atop hills on either side of the border fence just a few hundred metres from each other to 'meet' and speak to each other through megaphones. In this manner, they attend ceremonies like family weddings and the funerals of parents and siblings. Most will never be able to afford or be permitted to make the long journey around the border to actually meet or touch their families again.

Though the roots of this play lie in this extraordinary place, the play itself is neither political nor specifically located and moves into a deeply personal space involving a mother, her two children, their hidden histories and the separation of family by fences of varying definitions.

Cast

Aziz A man. Late thirties

Saira His sister, a few years younger

Mother Aziz and Saira's. Late fifties.

1. Character names may be changed as required.

2. Italicized lines denote that they are spoken through a megaphone.

3. The absence of any punctuation mark at the end of a sentence denotes that the delivery of the next line commences instantly.

4. A punctuation mark ' / ' denotes the point of commencement of the delivery of the next line.

5. A punctuation mark ' * ' denotes that the delivery of the line next marked ' * ' commences at that point.

6. A punctuation mark '//' denotes the commencement of the overlapping actions next marked '//'.

1

(A tacky hotel room in the middle of the desert. Outside, the sounds of a market)

Saira Fuck the line.

Aziz What happens if you cross it?

Saira You die.

Aziz Exactly. We'll be talking to her over a border. And a bloody dangerous one, at that, so

Saira So I want to get her out of there. And you don't want to die.

Aziz You want to?

Saira *(Pause)* Wouldn't kill me if I did. And I would have if she hadn't got us out of the country. And so would you.

Aziz She wouldn't want to get out if we died, would she?

Saira No.

Aziz So. The line. From here to... the lamp there, okay?

(Saira lights a cigarette)

Saira   All right.

Aziz   It's very important!

Saira   All right!

Aziz   Listen, if I crossed it and they shot me, she'd try even harder. For you. But if something happened to you it would finish her.

Saira   Whose fault is that?

Aziz   Yours but that's not the point. Thing is, we both want her out. To come back to England with us.

(Pause)

Saira   To be with us.

Aziz   Exactly.

Saira   To feel the love.

Aziz   The what?

Saira   The line.

Aziz   What about it?

Saira   Where is it? No. The real one, I mean. How do we know?

Aziz   The soldiers come and mark it every morning – a line of chalk in the sand. When they've finished they stroll into neutral territory and chat with each other.

Saira   How wide is it?

Aziz   The neutral bit?

Saira   How far from us to her?

Aziz	About half a kilometre.
Saira	Half a kilometre!
Aziz	Yes.
Saira	How do we talk?
Aziz	Megaphones.
Saira	You're joking!

(Aziz goes over to a bag and holds up a megaphone)

I don't believe this.

Aziz	You'd rather just wave?
Saira	It's just… how do we hear her?
Aziz	She knows. The soldiers' morning chat? They're not discussing the football, you know. How do you think I set this up in the first place? It's big business. Do you know how much they pay to be posted to this bit of the border? And it's even more over on our side.
Saira	You mean mum's side.
Aziz	Mum's side, sorry. Used to be ours.
Saira	Five years ago. Now this is ours, at least for the moment. And ours is hers.
Aziz	This isn't ours! We keep going to war with them, for Christ's sake! Get screwed each time.
Saira	That's what happens in wars, you know. Everyone gets screwed. Except the ones doing the screwing up.
Aziz	Oh, save it for your next demo. Should be enough to topple the government!

Saira   What and have you lot instead?

(Saira lights a cigarette)

Aziz   When are you going to give up?

Saira   Someday. Soon.

Aziz   When you die, perhaps?

Saira   No reason to then.

Aziz   Cheap stuff! I mean, you may as well do it properly if you're going to kill yourself.

Saira   That's a thought. *(Pause)* Unfortunately, I work for the cause, not the money.

Aziz   Work? Standing at street corners distributing appeals to save the Trans Siberian speckled earthworm is work?

Saira   Living off dad's slush money and trying to subvert the government back home is work?

Aziz   Yes, it bloody well is!

Saira   An investment, I suppose.

Aziz   Exactly.

Saira   So you can take over the place and make some money for yourself!

(Aziz laughs. Saira goes to the window, looks out, down to the sill)

Saira   Dead.

Aziz   What?

Saira   All. Dead. Hour after hour, beating themselves against a sheet of glass…*(Pause)* The insects.

Aziz   Ah.

Saira   And all because

Aziz   Someone nasty shut the window?

Saira   They thought there was only one way out.

(A muezzin's call to prayer goes up outside. Aziz ties a handkerchief to his head, unrolls a prayer mat and performs his Namaaz. Saira watches)

Saira   'In the name of God the Merciful, the Compassionate.

When the hypocrites come to thee they say: "We bear witness that thou art indeed the Messenger of God." And God *knows* that thou art indeed His Messenger, and He bears witness that the hypocrites are truly liars.

They use their faith as a disguise, and bar others from the path of God. Evil is what they do.

Because they have believed and then renounced their faith, therefore a seal has been set upon their hearts, so they are devoid of understanding.

(Saira lights her cigarette)

Equal it is for them, whether thou askest forgiveness for them or not; God will not forgive them. God guides not the people of the ungodly.

O believer, let not your riches nor your children divert you from God's remembrance: whoso doest that, they are the losers.

Give then, that which We have provided you before death befalls you, and you say "Reprieve me awhile, so I may give in charity, and so become one of the righteous."

But God will reprieve no soul when its term expires. And God is aware of the things you do.'

(She watches. Aziz finishes, rolls up the mat)

Aziz   So what was all that about?

Saira   The Koran. Chapter 63. 'The Hypocrites'.

Aziz   I'm supposed to be impressed? When I know you don't give a shit?

Saira   About?

Aziz   Your religion. Bet it's all wrong anyway.

Saira   Like your Namaaz performance

(He grins at Saira. They laugh)

I know the Book. That's why I don't need your 'religion'.

Aziz   Mm, I don't need it either, actually.

Saira   But

Aziz   But... it's needed of me.

(They smile)

Aziz   So how do we tell her?

Saira   What.

Aziz   What?

Saira   Tell her what?

Aziz   The plan.

Saira   You mean tell her.

Aziz   Without telling her.

Saira   Obviously.

(Pause)

Aziz   Well?

(Pause)

Saira   How should I know?

Aziz   Because you've done it for years, you and Mum.

Saira   What?

Aziz   Drivelled on in your stupid little codes. Now you can use it for something really important. Listen now: we need to tell her that the men will come on Friday night to get her out of the country and that she shouldn't resist. That they're there to help her. She mustn't resist.

Saira   You mean there's a use for our 'stupid little codes'?

Aziz   Sorry. But it was irritating. And rude. To us.

Saira   Rude? Rude?? I'll tell you what's rude: You don't call her in five years – that's rude. You call me for the first time in two – that's rude. You rush me here to meet Mum, and then it turns out you only really brought me along for my 'stupid little codes'– that's fucking rude!

Aziz   So tell me. How?

Saira   No you tell me .Why?

Aziz   And if I don't you'll walk out and go home, right?

(Pause)

Saira   Yes.

(Aziz strides to the door and gestures extravagantly)

Aziz   I'll give her your regards. No, I'll tell her how much you wanted to see her, but…

(Silence)

Exactly. Now, how?

(Pause)

Saira   Why can't you just call her?

Aziz   Oh brilliant! And I suppose we could also call the intelligence services and ask if they need any clarifications. As a courtesy.

(Pause)

So now. How can you tell her the plan. And to not resist.

(Pause)

Saira   One million ways. So many years trying to steer clear of trouble…

(Pause)

but most often…

(Pause)

most often…

Aziz   Most often? That's it, come on! Most often?

Saira	The one she… the best one… and the closest for this… 'When they come home pinching the bridges of their noses don't tell them to get their shoes off the carpet. Just let them do what they want.'

(Pause)

Aziz	Did either of you ever consider seeing a doctor?
Saira	He slapped me.
Aziz	The doctor?
Saira	Dad. He slapped me. He came home, flopped down and pinched his nose. Didn't even notice me. I went over and sat on the arm of his chair. I just told him he should get his shoes off, that's all!
Aziz	Why?
Saira	And he slapped me!
Aziz	Well…
Saira	Mum took me away and she told me that.
Aziz	Did she say 'them'?
Saira	Yes.
Aziz	'Them'?
Saira	You too, I suppose.
Aziz	I don't pinch my nose.
Saira	You just did.
Aziz	When?
Saira	When I finished saying that.

Aziz   That's because it's bloody useless! Dad died six years ago! And he slapped all of us all the time!

Saira   He slapped me just that once.

Aziz   Really? *(Pause)* Still...

Saira   She'll remember.

Aziz   Why? Just because he did it only once?

Saira   Because they fought about it.

Aziz   They fought about the weather, for god's sake!

Saira   And she hit him.

(Pause)

Aziz   Mum hit dad?

(Silence)

Saira   Mum and I have had the nose thing ever since. To tell each other to do nothing, not to resist

Aziz   When?

Saira   Oh, all the time. At dinner. Defending the servants if they got something wrong and dad was roasting them? She'd go Tap-Tap on her nose. Or when dad was talking politics or art or something with his guests and I interrupted

Aziz   With something stupid and naive. Yeah, I remember that!

Saira   Or too honest for you to have thought of.

Aziz   Please.

Saira   She'd go 'nosey, nosey'.

Aziz   Thank God!

Saira   All the time, really. Whenever she wanted me to back off. The thing is as good as an alarm clock! Trust me. Remember when they came for Dad?

Aziz   For fuck's sake, there was a gun at my head!

Saira   Remember I tried to

Aziz   I remember a gun at my head

Saira   I tried to go to him.

Aziz   Daft thing to do.

Saira   And they hit me. With a rifle butt.

Aziz   Well, what did you?

Saira   I tried to get up again. Mum screamed. Nose!

Aziz   Nose?

Saira   Yes. I sank back and looked up at her. And I was screaming Nose! Nose!

Aziz   Then they shot him and left. *(Breath)* The relief!

Saira   Did you hear what I said?

Aziz   Mmm? Nose, Nose?

Saira   And?

Aziz   And... dad died... and... well okay, it might work. Seems a bit dodgy, though they listen in on everything, watch for anything – a foreign language, things that don't make sense, things that make too much.

Saira   It will work! How long do we have?

Aziz   Half an hour before the next lot arrives.

Saira   The next lot?

Aziz   Yes. There are piles of them shouting all along the border, but this is a good quiet place and the sound travels well, or something. So there are slots. Now, how do we go about this so it doesn't seem strange?

Saira   We just talk, flow along, and I'll say it when it's right.

Aziz   And mum? I suppose you know how she'll respond, what she's going to say! What if...

Saira   We'll steer her there. Don't worry, it will be all right.

Aziz   What if

Saira   We'll start with the usual, of course

Aziz   Saira, what if

Saira   The helloes, how's so-and-so, the cats, the garden, blah blah blah

Aziz   What if

Saira   What if WHAT?

Aziz   What if she doesn't want to leave?

(Pause)

Saira   Why shouldn't she?

Aziz   Well... she's got some man, or something, I believe.

(Pause)

Saira   You know?

Aziz   I know everything I want to know.

Saira   And? You know who? When / they

Aziz   I don't want to know that! They keep trying to tell me, but I've warned them off. I don't want to know the pathetic details! And it's just a man! What chance does he have against the lure of little Saira!

(Pause)

Well, does he?

(Pause)

Saira   I think she'll come anyway.

Aziz   You sure? Why? They've split up?

Saira   You didn't want to know, remember?

(Pause)

Anyway, if she doesn't want to leave, what?

Aziz   What then?

Saira   Nothing I suppose. We just keep talking to her on the phone. And missing her.

Aziz   But

Saira   Caressing the wire. Trying to touch the voice that's trapped inside it.

Aziz   But

Saira   But what? How do you care! I'm not even sure why you are bothering with all this, considering how you feel about her! *(Pause)* It's me who died slowly, year after year, without her.

Aziz	So it's okay with you if she doesn't / want to leave?
Saira	It's not fucking okay, okay? She will want to! That's it. What's wrong with you!
Aziz	What if she just refuses? You know her, how contrary she can be. *(Pause)* She's become bloody important to us now!

(Pause)

Saira	What was that?
Aziz	What?
Saira	What did you just say?
Aziz	I mean, having her with us... it matters... to us.
Saira	That's not what you said.
Aziz	It is what I said.

(Pause)

Saira	You never say what you say you say, remember. From Dad's little black book of politics.
Aziz	You wouldn't understand it.
Saira	Of course.

(Pause)

	All right, let's do this. I'll be us, and you can be mum.
Aziz	That's a laugh!
Saira	Look, let's just try, okay? Hi mum!
Aziz	Saira! Darling!

Saira   Aziz is here too, mum.

Aziz   Oh. Hello Aziz.

Saira   For fuck's sake!

Aziz   All right, sorry.

Saira   Are you well Aziz?

Aziz   Great! I'm respectful, I wash behind my ears, and I wank twice a day.

(Aziz laughs. Saira doesn't)

              Okay, okay. Get on with it.

Saira   So, how are you, mum?

Aziz   I'm all right, dear.

Saira   Are you well?

Aziz   Yes, yes, fine.

Saira   Are you sure?

Aziz   For pity's sake, I said I'm fine! Absolutely.

Saira   Oh yes, 'for pity's sake' this and 'for pity's sake' that! Good one!

Aziz   Yes, no one bothers me. I'm guarded all the time anyway.

Saira   It didn't stop them with dad though, did it?

Aziz   No, but that made me impossible to touch.

Saira   So, how is Maria? Still producing banquets?

Aziz	I'm afraid so. She has to. Too many people in and out of the place all the time. With petitions and things. And the party work.

(Pause)

Saira	How's my room? Does the loo door still squeak? How's Judy? Still hanging from the bedpost?
Aziz	No dear.
Saira	You moved her? Where?
Aziz	Had to put her away.
Saira	Mum would never do that! And what is all this party shit? Mum is not political.
Aziz	Yeah, and I'm not mum. Get on with it. Your room is the office now.
Saira	What office? *(Pause)* All right, can you get Judy out of there for me somehow?
Aziz	It's just a toy koala, dear. I have more important things to think of. I'm not even sure I didn't throw it away. I'll have a look. No promises.

(Pause)

Saira	Do people come over every evening, then?
Aziz	Most
Saira	Who are you having over tonight?
Aziz	Just some people.
Saira	Anyone I know?

Aziz	Don't think so. The usual party workers, I suppose.
Saira	What about weekends? Friday, for example?
Aziz	Someone or the other, I suppose. There's too much to do to bother about that sort of thing.
Saira	So you're up till late usually?
Aziz	Depends. Till midnight most days.
Saira	And Maria still brings in your tea at six?
Aziz	Yes.
Saira	Every day?
Aziz	Yes
Saira	So you only have yourself to yourself between midnight and six.
Aziz	Yes.
Saira	Must be lonely.
Aziz	The nights? No different, really. I walked out of your father's room many years ago, you know.
Saira	He threw you out!
Aziz	I walked out. I just lost interest. I couldn't be bothered with him anymore.
Saira	That's not true!
Aziz	Who would know better, you or me?
Saira	Me!
Aziz	You were just a child then. Still are.

Saira   Mum wouldn't have said that!

Aziz   Well dear, there are a lot of things I should have said but didn't.

Saira   Like what?

Aziz   Like dad getting tired of your running into our bedroom every time you felt insecure.

Saira   There were just times I needed to… talk. To be with you.

Aziz   At two in the morning? Every other night? When you were eighteen??

(Pause)

Saira   You never said anything. He never said anything.

Aziz   Not to you, no.

(Pause)

Saira   To you?

Aziz   Yes.

Saira   What?

Aziz   He told me to sort it out or use another room. *(Pause)* I used another room.

Saira   So he threw you out.

Aziz   No child, he didn't. I made a choice. Perhaps the wrong one. Certainly the saddest. Because of you. But you can't see that, can you? What it did. To us.

Saira   You're lying!

Aziz   Am I? Perhaps. Still… did I get it right? Did I choose correctly? Did I perhaps… neglect my men?

Saira   He beat you! All the time! You said so yourself!

Aziz   Aziz. What about Aziz?

Saira   Aziz didn't give a toss. Still doesn't.

(Pause)

Aziz   Oh my child.

Saira   Anyway, its just men. *(Pause)* Remember what you used to tell me about them? About when they came in late at night pinching the bridges of their noses? Strange things, men. *(Pause)* Still, it's sad that it won't be like that again.

Aziz   Mmm

Saira   And then that night they came for dad, and you shouted 'Nose'.

Aziz   No.

Saira   What?

Aziz   It was 'No'. Nose, you imagined. It was ' No'.

Saira   I wanted to help dad. I really tried, didn't I?

Aziz   You couldn't have helped dad, dear. He was finished the minute they walked in.

I shouted to you because I didn't want

Saira   Well, I wasn't going to not try just because I could get hurt! I wasn't thinking of / myself

Aziz	They had a gun at Aziz's head
Saira	And
Aziz	A gun. At his head. AZIZ'S!!

(Pause)

Never struck you, did it? It was Aziz I was terrified for.

Saira	But it was me they hit!
Aziz	Yes, I suppose... but... I should know, dear. I was trying to save Aziz. Desperately. More than anyone else, he was the one in danger. More than anything else.
Saira	They hit me!
Aziz	They would never bother with a girl. You didn't matter. It would serve no purpose, and people might react... badly. I'm sorry. It's just the politics of assassination. It was Aziz I was worried for. It was always... Aziz.

(Pause)

Saira	Anyway, it's never going to happen again, thank God!
Aziz	No. It's just me now. Alone. No one to protect anymore.
Saira	And if they came again you'd know what to do, wouldn't you? They burst in, and you start fighting them. And I'd say 'Nose' and you'd understand.
Aziz	used to say that to you!
Saira	Yes. But just this once, for one day – Friday, say – I tell you, and *you* don't resist.
Aziz	Why?

Saira	Because if you care for us… for me… you should.
Aziz	Oh, don't worry, no one is coming for me. It's important that I'm safe for a lot of people now. Apart from you.
Saira	What people, mum?
Aziz	…people.
Saira	Which people?
Aziz	The people. In general. Everyone.
Saira	Everyone?
Aziz	Yes.
Saira	Mum?
Aziz	Oh, get on with it
Saira	Who?
Aziz	All of them! The whole damn country!

(Pause)

Saira	She is bloody important!
Aziz	Except the bastards who…
Saira	To us!
Aziz	Exactly… you see, she's… Are you eating well, dear?
Saira	A symbol!
Aziz	Are you getting along with your cousins? Is Aziz taking care of you or is he just being a nuisance as always?
Saira	Important to us…!
Aziz	Stop! You crossed the line!

Saira   I did not.

Aziz   You did!

Saira   They aren't ever straight. Like the people who draw them. I am in a bulge.

Aziz   All right, dear. I'll remember about your nose! Don't worry!

Saira   You fuck!

Aziz   Bye! Bye, dear!

Saira   You slimy, devious fuck!

Aziz   Shut up.

Saira   Don't

Aziz   Shut up, you stupid Bolshie bitch! If it is done right, she could change history! The whole bloody country's beating down her doors, and God knows how, but she can talk to them all with one word, touch them all with a gesture. For fuck's sake, what do you talk to her on the phone *about*??

Saira   Important things. Politics wasn't ever, for us.

(Pause)

Aziz   You really… don't you have any idea how big she is, do you?

Saira   I know how big she is to me. And I think I know how big she is to you! I mean, how could you have expected her to care for you at all? What, were you always like this? Before I came along?

Aziz   Before you came I didn't need to be.

(Pause)

Saira   So that's it. I get her back and you take her away from me again! And I have to share her, not just with you but the million other bastards around you! I won't do it!

(Aziz moves to placate her)

Fuck off!

Aziz   You'd rather leave her there? Never see her again?

(Saira is in tears)

Saira   Yes! Maybe yes! I'll find a way to her.

(Pause)

A way. Out.

(Pause. She goes to the window, gazes at the struggling insects)

There's always a way. You just need to see it.

(Pause)

Aziz   Listen

Saira   No!

Aziz   You'll be able to touch her...

Saira   Go. Please!

Aziz   She'll hold you and you feel the warmth of

Saira   Go away! Leave me alone!

(Pause)

Saira   I hate you! I hate this whole damn… everything.
            Everything.

(Silence)

Aziz   Look, it works for both of us. You have your reasons, I
             have mine.

Saira   This is your *mother*! You call that… 'reasons'??

Aziz   And yours are wonderful?

Saira   At least they are pure!

Aziz   Purely selfish.

Saira   Because I care for mum?

Aziz   Yes. And I'm a bastard because I care for a whole fucking
             country.

Saira   You don't care for a country. You love the idea that you
             care for a country. You can't love a country.

Aziz   Why not?

Saira   It's not as though it talks to you, has dinner with you,
             smells of lavender soap and crochet thread when it
             holds you, cherishes you. Loves you back.

Aziz   No?

Saira   No. It's just a bloody… idea. Cooked up in someone's
             head. It wouldn't even exist if someone hadn't decided
             to say it was there, put down those *(pointing at the line)*.
             And if you *(rubs out the line with her feet)* it's gone.

Aziz   Okay look, forget it. Just think of it: touching the
             dimple on her chin, laying with her twirling her
             necklace, tracing that funny scar on her arm…

(Saira turns away distraught. She sits heavily and stares at the floor a long while. She looks up)

Saira So.

Aziz Look, I'm sorry, but that's the way it is. Your whole… system needs her, so does mine. We have no choices here Saira, you know that.

(Pause)

Aziz Now, we should have a backup. What if we don't get anywhere with this nose pinching thing?

Saira We will

Aziz What about the snake? I mean she couldn't ever forget that! There was this time once when mum and I were down in the garden. Alone. Just her and me. And this snake

Saira Yeah, yeah I know.

Aziz Mm?

Saira You told me about it. Many, many times. How it suddenly appeared and

Aziz Suddenly it was there, all over me!

Saira I'm sleepy now.

Aziz She'll remember that!

Saira I'm turning in.

Aziz And she smiled.

Saira Where's my toothbrush?

Aziz   she just stood there! I know

Saira   I'm sure I chucked it in somewhere.

Aziz   she stood there and smiled.

Saira   Yeah, well, I asked her about it.

(Saira stops rummaging about in her bag and surfaces with a toothbrush. She exits. Sounds off-stage of running water)

Aziz   I mean, it was a big thing. She'd remember it. It was wrapped around

Saira   *(Off)* Ooh! It's fucking cold!

Aziz   All around me!

Saira   *(Off)* There's no bloody hot water.

Aziz   In seconds her son could be dead.

Saira   *(Off)* Listen Aziz…

Aziz   And she did NOTHING!

Saira   *(Off)* She said…

Aziz   Nothing. Just stood there. No reaction. As though it didn't matter if… maybe if we brought the conversation around to how if

(Saira enters)

Saira   Aziz…

Aziz   …if anyone comes and threatens

Saira   There was no snake.

Aziz   What?

| Saira | It never happened. She said it never. Happened. |

(Pause)

| Aziz | It did! Really! |

(Pause)

| | It did. She'll remember. She did nothing. *(Pause)* No resistance. No resistance at all. She must remember! |

(Silence)

| Saira | She won't. Just some child's fancy, many years ago. |
| Aziz | No! Listen, please… |

(Pause)

| Aziz | We still need a backup plan. |

(Pause)

Saira	I have one.
Aziz	What?
Saira	Can't tell you.
Aziz	What do you mean?
Saira	Can't tell you. It would spoil it.
Aziz	I don't need to be entertained. What is it?
Saira	It needs you to react to it. Spontaneously.
Aziz	Look…
Saira	She will understand the nose pinching thing anyway. She will. Don't worry. *(Pause)* And if… if she doesn't… this one she wouldn't ever forget. Ever. Trust me. Now it's late, I am tired.

Aziz   What do I do? Do you need me to do anything?

Saira   Just be yourself.

Aziz   I don't like it. Are you sure?

Saira   It's… too… big to not work. But you're not a part of it.

Aziz   What??

Saira   At this point, I mean. Now good night.

(Saira settles down to sleep. Aziz stares, then exits. Sounds off-stage of a flush, water running. Aziz enters)

Aziz   The thing is… the thing is… look… you think I'm enjoying this…

Saira   I don't know, Aziz… it's late…

Aziz   This… using mum. This

Saira   Mmm

Aziz   Look, it isn't as if I don't care for her, as if… Saira?… Saira? Asleep. As if it doesn't hurt that I never had mum to care, didn't want mum to care, need… *(Pause)* dreaming of knights, no doubt. Saira always dreamed about knights. Great big shiny ones. All doing great things. Their mighty steeds, their quivering lances. Freud never got to that one, did he? Or did he? Always knights. And always asleep in ma's arms. And I… I dreamed about… snakes. And the one that wrapped itself around me that afternoon. In the sunlight at the bottom of the garden. One minute she was telling me not to trouble the snails, the next, there it was.

Climbing my leg. Till it was all over me. Without a sound, without anyone noticing. Invaded! And I stood and stared. Ma had frozen. And then... she smiled! She smiled! She could have done a thousand things. But she just... smiled. Like she was in shock. But I knew she wasn't. Because then she turned and walked away. I stood there shivering, waiting for the end. And then it just lazily glided off me and up a tree. Disappeared without a sound. As though I was too worthless to waste its power upon. I sank to the ground. That's how they found me. Mum rushed to me, as though she had just seen me... this... shattered... wreck. Her voice was trembling, with terror, with guilt, I don't know. I looked up at her, stripped of dignity. Little. Then I managed to get up. And run away. From her. *(Pause)* In the dream she goaded the snake with a stick. And I was crying, shouting, sobbing. Goading and screaming and sobbing and goading. I woke up so often that way. And I could never go to her. Because then she'd see me the same way she saw me that afternoon. Little. Afraid. Worthless. And she would offer me nothing. Again. And anyway Saira always seemed to be with her at night. *(Pause)* Strange I should need her so much now, that it should ever become so... important to me.

2

(A slash of dawn across the room. Saira stirs.)

Saira   Aziz? *(She fumbles for the time, rolls over, stares at the ceiling, then at Aziz)* The sleep of the accepted. It's his world. It understands him. Admires him, his way of thinking, his deals with it. With how he deals with himself. He is not here to get mum out. He is here to get what he needs. Fast asleep. No dreams. Dreaming is our cross. Ours, the jokers on the pavement, the ones to smirk at on the way to the office. The ones with nothing more useful to do than try and save the world. It's too late for us now. Or maybe just too early. I'm so tired. We are all so tired. The people on their way to office, they don't see the exhaustion. They just look at the dark circles and the hunted faces and shiver and push on quickly, like we might have a disease or something. Never thinking it's just… exhaustion. And we are all so tired because… when we sleep, we dream. And this is not a world for dreaming. This time is not for us. It's his time. Aziz's time. I'm so tired of dreaming. I just want to… sleep. No dreams. No conscience. No battles to keep it. No mornings to dread. Just dead. Dark… sleep. Maybe. Maybe soon.

(A muezzin's call)

Aziz! Aziz, wake up! It's time.

3

(*A silvery, thin early morning light over a vast open space. Saira and Aziz enter*)

Saira   Jesus what's that stink?

(*Aziz unfolds his handkerchief and ties it round his head*)

Aziz   That's

Saira   You're going to pray again??

Aziz   No

Saira   Good.

(*She snatches the handkerchief and ties it over her nose*)

Aziz   Mmm, suits you. You look like a… believer.

(*Saira quickly gives it back*)

Saira   Yeesh! What is it??

Aziz   A body. There, look. In no man's land. Rotting.

Saira   For fuck's sake, can't they take it away??

Aziz   The place is mined.

Saira   God.

Aziz   Here. Come over here. It doesn't smell here, somehow.

(*Aziz wears the handkerchief. Saira stares.*)

What?? She's looking for it! Easier to identify us.

(Aziz scans the landscape through binoculars. Saira stands beside him, megaphone in hand)

Saira	Can you see her?
Aziz	No. No sign yet.
Saira	Where is she?
Aziz	There! There she is!
Saira	Where? What is she wearing?
Aziz	White.

(Pause)

Saira	And the scarf?
Aziz	No scarf.
Saira	No scarf?
Aziz	No.
Saira	Are you sure it is her?
Aziz	Yes. No scarf! Wonder what made her / stop
Saira	*Mum! Mum!…mum! It's me!*
Mother	*Saira? Is that you?*
Saira	*Mum! Yes, mum! It's me!*
Mother	*Saira darling! How are you?*
Saira	*Fine, mum! Aziz is here too!*
Mother	*Hello son.*

(Aziz takes off the handkerchief)

Aziz   Hello mum. Round one to me.

Mother   *Saira are you all right?*

Aziz   Give it to me!

Saira   *No!*

Mother   *No?*

Saira   *No mum, I was talking to Aziz.*

Mother   *No point saying no to him. Trust me. Are you well, Aziz?*

Aziz   Lovely. I wash behind my ears, I'm respectful to my elders, and

(Saira moves to cover his mouth)

              I *(shouting)* wank twice a day!

Mother   *What?*

Saira   *He says he loves you. How are things at home?*

Mother   *Er... fine dear, fine.*

Saira   Good, good...

(Pause)

Aziz   Well, go on! Maria, Judy, remember?

Saira   I...

Aziz   Okay let me give it a go.

(Aziz takes the megaphone)

              And Maria? Is she still getting those huge dinners together?

Mother *She's left.*

(Pause)

Aziz *Oh, why?*

Mother *Things.*

Aziz Bye bye double chocolate mousse cake.

(Saira takes the megaphone)

Saira *Who's cooking now?*

Mother *…we have another cook.*

Aziz As good as Maria?

Saira It doesn't matter.

Aziz Doesn't it?

Mother *He's quite a good cook actually.*

Aziz Okay, that's enough. Give me that. *(Grabs the megaphone)So Mum, how are things?*

Mother *Everything's well. Could be better, but I can't really complain.*

Aziz *Good, good. I believe you have a man!*

Saira Give me that!

(Aziz evades her)

Mother *Now dear, please!*

Aziz *Have I said a word? Have I said a thing?*

Mother *Look, I know*

Saira Aziz, please! Leave it.

Aziz   *It's all right.*

(Pause)

Mother   *What did you say?*

Aziz   *It's all right.*

Mother   *You mean...*

Aziz   *I mean it's all right.*

(Pause)

Mother   *You don't know what you've just done.*

Aziz   *What?*

Mother   *You don't know how happy you've made me! All these lonely years...*

Aziz   *Why, what have I*

Mother   *Thank you for not asking why*

Aziz   *Nah, it's all right.*

Mother   *For not judging me.*

Aziz   *Why should I?*

Mother   *You know, he's*

Aziz   *It's okay! I mean, I am sure he's nice. But I don't need to know about him, what he eats, his name and number...*

(Pause)

Mother   *Oh.*

Aziz   *Are you entertaining a lot, then?*

(Pause)

Mother *No.*

Aziz *Just the evenings, I suppose?*

Mother *No. I'm exhausted by then. There's suddenly so much to do. I don't really know why.*

Saira Give it to me!

Aziz *What for?* I can do this too, /you know

Mother *Oh, there are so many people who seem to think I'm... useful.*

Saira *(Snatches the megaphone)* It has to be done slowly. Naturally. *Really? What people, mum? Anyone interesting?*

Mother *Well, mostly scroungers and politicians who think I can be used. But also some good people. Charities. Intellectuals.*

Aziz Intellectuals! Mum! / Hah!

Mother *You have to help if you can. Helping everyone else is all I've ever done anyway. And before I knew it, I became some sort of... figure.*

Saira *You're a public figure?*

Aziz Give me that!

Saira *What sort?*

Aziz A huge fucking national rallying point of sorts!

Saira And they allow that? Why?

Mother *I... I don't know. People seem to... there's dust all over the paintings, and the silver's all tarnished and... it's all* *falling apart. I don't know. I haven't done any crocheting for months now. It's…*

(Pause)

I miss it. I miss not having to wonder why everyone is trying so hard to be nice to me. I miss the honesty. I miss my own.

(Pause)

Is it cold in London, Saira?

(Long pause)

Saira   *Yes. But it's warmer down in Italy.*

Aziz   Italy.

Mother   *I think of it so often, Italy.*

Aziz   Italy? What are you, fucking nutters?

Saira   *Seriously?*

(Pause)

Mother   *Yes.*

(Pause)

Aziz   What are you on about!?

Saira   Just another stupid little code!

Aziz   About?

Mother   *It's so cold, Saira.*

Saira   *It'll turn.*

Mother   *When?*

Saira *Soon. Soon now.*

(Aziz snatches the megaphone)

Aziz *You have security people? At night?*

Mother *Yes. Watching over me all the time. Why?*

Aziz *Because when they come…*

(Saira snatches at the megaphone)

Saira You're going too fast!

Aziz *Will you shut the fuck up?*

Mother *That's disgusting, Aziz!*

Aziz *So / tomorrow…*

Mother *Apologize to her.*

Aziz *Tomorrow when * they / come…*

Saira You're not making sense! They're watching!

Mother **Apologize!*

Mother *Apologize!*

Aziz *Sorry. Are you entertaining tomorrow?*

Mother *Oh for pity's sake! We're staying in, since it is so important to you.*

(Pause)

Aziz *Good.*

Mother *Yes I… play chess in the evening most days.*

Saira Chess?

Aziz   *Chess? With whom?*

Saira   With him.

Aziz   Mum? Chess?? She must be awful!

Mother *I don't really enjoy it. I'd so prefer to be knitting or… but I suppose if it makes him…*

Aziz   *He makes you play chess, sacks your help, has you watched day and night… doesn't sound like much fun to me!*

Saira   Leave it. It is her life now.

(She lunges for the megaphone. Aziz evades her and trips away)

Aziz   *I mean, you could just give him the finger! You're good at that.*

Mother *What?*

Aziz   *Doesn't matter.*

(Pause)

Mother *It was a deal.*

Aziz   *What deal? You did a deal??*

Mother *My whole life has been a deal, Aziz.*

Aziz   *So, what deal?*

(Pause)

Mother *Doesn't matter.*

Aziz   *What deal!?*

(Pause)

Mother *To get the two of you out of here.*

Saira   Mum!

Aziz   *We had a benefactor?? Who?*

Mother   I sold

Aziz   *We should reward him*

Mother   my choices.

Aziz   *So who is it?*

(Pause)

         Well, come on!

(Pause)

Saira   Just leave it Aziz .You said you didn't need to know.

Aziz   No wait, something tells me I should. *Mum?*

(Pause)

         What's going on? Tell us, mum. Go on. Who? Someone we know?

(Pause)

Mother   *Yes.*

Aziz   *Oh, good! And?*

Mother   *It's not important...*

Aziz   *Okay, then tell me. Who?*

Saira   Listen...

Aziz   *Go on, I'm listening.*

Mother   *His name is Hamid, if you want to know.*

Aziz   *Can't say I know him. The only Hamid I can think of is the cunt who sent them for dad.*

(Pause)

            Mum?

Saira   Give me that.

(Saira grabs at the megaphone)

Aziz   You mean...

            (Pause)

            No.

(Pause)

            No!

Saira   Yes.

Aziz   Fuck! Fuck, fuck, fuck, FUCK!!

Mother   *I heard that.*

Aziz   Well good for you, you sick old slag!!

Saira   *Mum...*

Aziz   You knew? He had dad killed! *(He snatches the megaphone)* He killed dad!

(Pause)

Mother   *Yes. I know.*

Saira   And dad was quite happy trying to do the same to him. You know that.

(Pause. Saira takes the megaphone)

Aziz   She did a deal with him! What kind of person

Saira   *Mum?*

Mother   *Yes.*

Saira   *Do you love him?*

Mother   *When you get older love becomes a much simpler word,
              Saira.*

Saira   *Do you love him, ma?*

(Pause)

Mother   *It wasn't required of me.*

Saira   *Are you happy?*

(Pause)

Mother   *It doesn't matter. Never did.*

(Aziz snatches the megaphone)

Aziz   *He forced you into this, didn't he?*

Mother   *No.*

Aziz   *Blackmail, I suppose. Or threats. Said he'd put you away
              like he did dad if you didn't... you know...*

Mother   *No!*

Aziz   *Then what? Why??*

Mother   *He was nice.*

(Pause)

Aziz   *You like the bastard?*

Mother   *Never thought about it.*

Aziz   *You sick, sick... bitch!*

Mother   *He's never hit me.*

Saira   And he's quite sexy.

Aziz   *Oh great!*

Mother   *I'm so glad you understand, Aziz.*

Aziz   *I wasn't talking to you!* Pervie bitches! One lives with him, the other wants to shag him!

Saira   That's not what I said.

Aziz   *Do you sleep with him?*

Saira   For God's sake!

Mother   *I'm fifty-seven. He's older. It's not important.*

Aziz   *It's not important that you sleep with him?*

Mother   *Not important if. And that, for that matter.*

Aziz   *So do you?*

Mother   *It makes no difference!*

Aziz   *So have you? Do you stay with him sometimes? In the same house? The same... room?*

Mother   *Sometimes. Whenever he wants.*

Aziz   *Like school kids. Rutting whenever you can! Where?*

Mother   *At home.*

Aziz   *Whose? Mine?*

Mother   *Mine.*

Aziz   *Is he good in bed, then, Mama?*

Mother   *Please Aziz.*

Aziz   *Then what!? Why?*

Mother   *What is not important. Why's easy.*

Aziz   *And our help... Maria all the others, they serve him? Do his clothes, bring him his food... is that why Maria left?*

Mother   *It's*

Aziz   *It is, isn't it?*

Mother   *Hamid has his preferences, his own...*

Aziz   *It's your house!*

Mother   *He insists he pays for things.*

Aziz   *A keep!*

(Pause)

Mother   *Perhaps.*

Aziz   *That's okay with you?*

Mother   *Everything is okay! And you know why everything is okay? Because*

I see you over there, that's why!

Aziz   *How many others does he have?*

(Pause)

Well? Does he? What about that actress slag who's always around him of late? And when he's abroad

Mother   *It's okay! It's... useful. It makes me even more... respected.*

Aziz   Well, well!

(Saira grabs the megaphone)

Saira   *Mom!*

Mother   *Sorry, love. It's the way the world is.*

Saira   *Mom! No! It's not...stop smirking! It's not you!*

Aziz   In the end it's a little bit of everybody, love. One day, even you.

Mother   *No. It isn't. I see myself, I hear myself talk, and... it's someone else. Someone who counts much more than the stitches on her needles. And has less at the end of the day. So if being a keep makes people love me more, it's okay. If it means making my children safe, it's okay. And it's the reason I could be here today.*

(Aziz snatches the megaphone)

Aziz   *They know about this?*

(Pause)

   They know we're here??

(Pause)

Saira   Oh shit! *(Takes the megaphone)* Mom, do they know you're seeing us just now?

Mother   *Yes.*

(Aziz grabs the megaphone)

Aziz   *You stupid... stupid... cow! Do you know the danger it could put us in?*

Mother   *Well, Saira is not a threat...*

Aziz	*And me? What about fucking ME!?*
Mother	*He would never harm you.*
Aziz	*Are you mad?? I could be in someone's gun-sights right now, for fuck's sake!*
Mother	*He loves / you.*
Aziz	*I could be... what?*
Mother	*He loves you.*
Aziz	*Oh, he told you that, did he?*
Mother	*No.*
Aziz	*So how do you know?*
Mother	*He does. I know.*
Aziz	She knows.
Mother	*I had five years to do it. To make you safe from him.*
Aziz	It's official: she's mad.
Mother	*The way he looks when we talk about you. The way he talks about you. I know him. I know him better than your father.*
Aziz	*I am his enemy!!*
Mother	*Oh, he knows that. But he's older now. Bit by bit. Sitting in the evenings playing chess. Talking about my life, the people who matter to me. You. So often, you. Bit by bit, I made him love you, Aziz.*
Aziz	You're not qualified to do that.

Mother *The little things. Things you did as a child. Times you were exposed. Lonely. Funny. Alone in your huge room, talking to a broken old car. Little things like that, things I had forgotten, things I learnt to love again too. Things that time takes away.*

Saira Give me * that.

Aziz Wait.

Mother * *Bit by bit, he discovered you. I did too. Began to understand the way you are.*

Aziz *Both of you? Me?*

Saira Give it to me!

(Aziz keeps the megaphone out of her reach)

Mother *Oh I know that you can hate, and hurt… we all do, in our own ways. But it's not you. Maybe… you only needed to have been… instead…*

Aziz *Mum?*

Mother *Maybe I…*

Aziz *Mum? What, mum? Needed to have what?*

(Saira grabs the megaphone)

Saira *You're sure he won't harm Aziz?*

Mother *He loves Aziz. I made him.*

Saira *And it's beyond him to kill someone he loves? There's no reason to believe that, is there?*

Mother *He's more open now to… looking hard at the sum of his life's calculations, what they've brought him. Aziz is safe. I* *made it safe for him. Five years it took. Five. Years. But I did it.*

Saira   *So are you any good at chess?*

Mother   *Not really. Too much plotting. I just want… nothing.*

(*Saira hands back the megaphone*)

Saira   She's not going to be any use as your huge fucking national rallying point now, is she?

Aziz   *Mum…*

Saira   Can we just get on with it now? We do still want her out, don't we?

Aziz   Of course. Mum'll help, you'll see.

Saira   You've got her wrong again. She's not interested. Can't you see?

Aziz   I'll talk to her…

Saira   She's beyond you. Again.

Aziz   I could convince her.

Saira   Really? And when did you last manage that?

Mother   *Are you still there?*

(*Aziz hands back the megaphone*)

Aziz   You do it. And quick. Will she come or not?

Saira   She's not going to help you even if she does, you know.

Aziz   That's my problem.

Saira   *Mum*

Mother   *Yes dear*

Saira   *Do you manage to spend a lot of time with him?*

Mother   *As much as he wants.*

Saira   *And is that a lot?*

Mother: *Can't tell anymore.*

Saira   *The evenings I suppose?*

Mother   *Yes if he's not busy with engagements. Sometimes we meet after he finishes.*

          Sometimes he's delayed with... and then we don't.

Saira   *Do you go to his place?*

(Pause)

Mother   *No.*

Saira   *Why not?*

Mother   *It's not... required.*

Saira   *Why?*

Mother   *It's just not. It is not my territory. Too many people around – the wrong ones. It would hurt me.*

Saira   *He's good to you?*

Mother   *Yes, he is.*

Saira   *But different homes, different...*

Mother   *I stopped wishing a long time ago, Saira. And it would hurt what I do.*

Saira   *You love what you do so much?*

Mother   *Can we just let this be? I don't know what I love! I don't know what I should be doing. I just. Don't. Want.... He comes over.*

Saira   *Just like that*

Mother   *Yes. Everyone knows. But going over to his place, that's different. I don't know why.*

Saira   *Are there days when he's definitely free? Holidays, Friday, for example.*

Mother   *He tries to keep Friday free. I do too. After dinner we play something. He stays late.*

Aziz   Good! A gun at his fucking temple! And she won't be able to resist them then, will she?

Saira   *So you'll be together tomorrow, then.*

Mother   *Tomorrow, yes. We'll be meeting tomorrow. And we'll chat and cook and be happy... a bit. Like when I drained him of his anger against Aziz. That made me happy, doing that. And hearing your voices about the house in the old days, talking to you. Making sure things were right, in their place. That made me happy too. (Pause) But you know, all the time it gnaws away at you, this being somehow... unrealized: like some painting that God abandoned halfway through and left to colour itself. What point do these little happinesses have, except to remind you that you forgot to paint in a big, real one for yourself? There's only so much you can get out of making sure everyone else is fine.*

Saira   *You were always there for us mom. That's a big thing!*

Aziz   Were you listening to her at all?

Mother   *Yes. For Aziz too.*

Aziz   Can't say I noticed, ma.

Mother   *You never noticed! Why?*

Aziz   It doesn't matter. You did all right.

Mother   *And I was there for your father, and for Hamid, and for a million people in general now. That's what I should be happy about? It's not that I'm not, except...*

(Pause)

          So tired. So...tired.

Saira   *Mum. Mum?*

Mother   *I'm still here.*

Saira   *Listen to me.*

Mother   *I am.*

Saira   *Listen very carefully. You could go to Italy quite easily.*

Aziz   Italy again! Oh fuck this!

Saira   *Did you hear me, mum? It's just a step away.*

Aziz   What's going on?

Saira   *Mum.*

(Pause)

Aziz   The back up?

(Pause)

Mother *I'll be able to crochet?*

Saira *All you like.*

Mother And not bother about anyone else?

Saira *Just you and me.*

Mother Maybe do some painting.

Saira *No one else.*

(Pause)

Mother Sleep without fear.

Saira *The sun on our backs.*

Mother *No distances to bridge then.*

Saira *No tunnels to trudge through.*

Mother *With only dull grey light at the end of them.*

Saira *Grey where we entered, grey at the end.*

Mother *Pushing forward through the darkness in between.*

Saira *Never upwards, or outwards.*

Mother *And the cold*

Saira *And the rain*

Mother *And the cold, rained on faces*

Saira *Not there.*

(Pause. Saira starts moving.)

Aziz What're you doing?

Saira get away from the line.

Mother	*And*
Saira	*And me*
Mother	*The sun. At peace.*
Aziz	What the hell… what are you doing?? Get back!
Saira	*Yes. You ready mum?*

(Pause)

Mum?

Mother	*Yes*
Saira	*You sure?*
Mother	*As I ever was. But you… you're young… your life*
Saira	Is mine. It's mine, mum. *Yes, I'm sure.*
Aziz	You've crossed it! You're over the line!!
Saira	Yes.
Aziz	Get back!!
Saira	I'm going to meet mum.
Aziz	Please! Listen…
Saira	There's always a way Aziz. You just have to see it.

(Saira throws the megaphone calmly into no man's land)

Aziz	What have you done??! Shit, She's moving! MUM? IT'S OKAY, MUM! NO NEED TO…. GET BACK! PLEASE! LISTEN, I'M
	What have you done! What have you done!

(He attacks the line, then stops)

MUM! CAN YOU HEAR ME?

Mother   Five years of death.

(Aziz paces the line, frantic)

Aziz   Oh God!

Mother   With my husband's killer.

Saira   It's going to be okay.

Mother   Living loveless.

Aziz   IT'S GOING TO BE OKAY, MUM!

Mother   Between life and… somewhere else.

Aziz   IT'S JUST…

Mother   To make you safe.

(She stops and looks down at the line)

Aziz   THERE'S SO MUCH WE HAVE TO

Mother   My work is done. If anyone noticed.

(She steps forward)

Aziz   So much! Oh God, no! You bitch!

(Shouting. Urgent, agitated voices over a megaphone bark out warnings)

Aziz   Come on Saira, don't be daft! You'll meet her soon enough!

Saira   On my terms. On our terms. Free to

(The megaphone continues to bark out warnings)

Aziz   Get back! Get back mum! Oh shit! Stop! Fucking /
            stop!

*(The voices over the megaphones become increasingly intimidating
and urgent)*

Aziz   No! Please! Saira! Oh God! Get back here!

Saira   What for? What are you offering me? What have you
            ever offered anybody?

*(A constant stream of screams and warnings from the soldiers continues
over the dialogue. Mounting hysteria as they move forward)*

Aziz   Mum! Please! No! / Please.

Mother   Bye Aziz.

Aziz   No!

*(A single shot rings out. Saira looks down at her feet, looks up in the
direction from where it came, smiles and continues walking.)*

Aziz   No! Please! They only want to meet! Please! Please!
            They only want to touch! // No! Oh God, No!! Oh
            God! Only want to be together! Together...

*(//a volley of distant shots. Mother stumbles as she is hit by bullets in
the chest, back. Two closer shots. Saira is hit in the stomach and head.
They both fall to the ground. The gunfire stops)*

            What for? What for??

*(Mother and Saira rise, leaving behind bloody shawls, jackets. Their
bodies, faces are torn and broken but their movements are effortless,
their demeanour uplifted. Saira turns swiftly and walks across to
Aziz. She touches him gently.)*

Saira   Thank you. *(Pause)* For caring. A bit.

Aziz   You're dead!

(Saira nods and walks away towards her mother)

You're dead!!

Mother *(Takes a light step)* A step. *(takes another step)* A step. *(takes another)* Another. *(takes another step)* And another! And another! And another and another and another *(she is tripping lightly round and round as she repeats the phrase over and over. She stops suddenly)* They're mine! All mine! Because *I* want to take them. When it began, my father held my feet and told me where to put them. Then my husband… didn't care, so where, how they went didn't matter anyway. Then they just went where they were told to. The one I took across that line? The first one of my life I took because *I* wanted to. *(Pause)* So now you know my whole life.

Aziz   Dead!

Mother Yes, Aziz. And you?

Aziz   Dead! Mad! Both of you. Mad!

Mother You?

Aziz   I'm alive! *(Pinching his arm)* Alive!!

Mother No Aziz. Not in a long, long time.

Aziz   Alive!

Mother I can't really remember when you were.

Aziz   Shut up! Shut. Up!!

Saira   So many lines!

Mother	The ones he drew for you
Saira	The ones you drew with him.
Mother	The one life draws for you
Saira	The ones we formed at school
Mother	Broke in college.
Saira	The ones at the… shops.
Mother	Between the cashier and your money.
Saira	Between buying and just taking
Mother	Or wanting and actually buying.
Saira	The ones across which bullets can fly.
Mother	And the fear of the bullets
Saira	Or of flying.
Aziz	What a load of shit!
Mother	Another line.
Aziz	I'm alive! And you're dead!
Saira	And another.
Aziz	Go away! You're dead!
Mother	Yes. And you are talking to us.
Aziz	This is not happening.
Saira	Of course. It *can't* be happening.
Aziz	Alive!!

Mother   What happened to you Aziz? Where did you go? And when? I suppose you were too little to be able to remember.

Aziz   Dead! Because you crossed it!

Saira   Crossed what?

Aziz   That! This!!

Saira   There's nothing there.

(Aziz picks up a fistful of chalk and flings it at them)

Aziz   There!!

(Pause till it disperses)

Mother   Where?

(Pause)

Aziz   How could you do this!? It was so important...

Mother   There was something in my head, you know. But it disappeared when Hamid happened. And then... it didn't matter anymore. Because I didn't have to care about what anyone thought. And you know, it's funny, but when I did that people began to notice. To respect that. To respect me. Because of it.

Aziz   It was so important! You're so important.

(Pause)

Aziz   I needed you. Just this once, ever, in my whole life, I needed you.

(Pause)

Mother What did you say?

(Pause)

Aziz …out. I needed you out.

(Pause)

Mother Why, son? Why did you need me out? I'm dead. You can say what you want.

Tell me.

Saira To use you, mum.

Mother Tell me son. Was there anything you needed to say? Maybe needed me to.

Needed to do…

Aziz Together.

Saira Engineer a coup of course!

Aziz It was so big. You were… so… big.

Mother For whom?

Saira A country.

Mother For whom? Son?

(Silence. Aziz walks about the line, kicking up dust)

Aziz It doesn't matter now. You're dead.

Mother Yes. But think of this: / since I'm dead…

Aziz If you're dead…

Mother …you can tell me.

Aziz   If you're dead, you're dead!! Don't you understand?? I left it too late!

(Saira turns to leave. Mother gestures her to a halt. Pause)

Aziz   I... why didn't you...

Mother   Go on.

Aziz   I never... I never meant... I didn't know how...

Saira   Take your time!

Mother   Go on.

Saira   Yes, we'll just settle down here while you compose your confession.

Aziz   Confession? What confession? I'm not confessing! Confess what? You're mad, both of you!

(Silence)

Mother   I'm leaving.

Saira   Yes, let's go. No point hanging about

Mother   Alone.

Saira   What?

Mother   I'm leaving alone.

Saira   Why? What did I do??

Mother   Nothing. Nothing much, really. You crossed over, yes, but... nothing much.

Really.

Saira   I killed myself! For you!

Mother   You killed yourself so you wouldn't have to grow up. At least Aziz lives with the lines. You just run away from them. Now's your chance, Saira.

Aziz   Mom! Wait!

Mother   You coming?

Aziz   Yes... mom, I... wait... talk to me... a bit.

Mother   You can come with me, you know.

Aziz   I *(he moves forward, stops)*... I'd like...

Mother   We can talk...

Aziz   I'd... really...

Mother   and talk, and...

Aziz   I really... don't... no.

(Pause)

Mother   It's all right.

Aziz   Yes

Mother   I'm so happy. I tried. You too. Hard.

Aziz   Yes. Thank you.

Mother   Good luck, little ones. I'll miss you so much.

(She begins to leave)

Saira   Wait. Mum!

(Mother leaves)

    MUM!!! Why did you do this? Why? What do I do now?

(Pause. She fishes about her clothes, finds a cigarette.)

Where's my bloody lighter?

(She looks about her pockets and pulls out a lighter. She flicks it on and looks at her face, as if into a mirror.)

Jesus, I look a mess!

(She pats her hair down, wipes her face. She looks around and finds a water hole. She kneels, puts her cigarette down carefully and dips her whole head in. She surfaces, her eyes closed. She opens them and looks out into the distance. She picks up the cigarette, takes a drag, gazes at the cigarette.)

I really need to give up this shit.

(She chucks the cigarette away and resumes gazing resolutely into the distance. Aziz has meanwhile sat heavily on the ground at the line. He kicks desultorily at it, then re-draws it, kicks and re-draws, kicks and re-draws... he is smiling.)

FADE TO BLACK